SAOL

THOUGHTS
FROM
IRELAND
ON LIFE
AND LIVING

CATHERINE CONLON lectures in Epidemiology
and Public Health at University College Cork.
Her keen interest in holistic health gave rise to
her book *Sonas: Celtic Thoughts on Happiness*
(2009), which explored the depths beneath the
distractions of modern life. A mother of four
living in Cork, she cites winning the Young
Scientist Award in 1981 as a turning point,
making her realise she could do anything if
she wanted it enough. She also published a
novel, *Valentia*, about island life off the coast
of Kerry.

This book is for
RAY
who is always on my side.

SAOL

THOUGHTS FROM IRELAND ON LIFE AND LIVING

C ATHERINE C ONLON

The Collins Press

FIRST PUBLISHED IN 2014 BY
The Collins Press
West Link Park
Doughcloyne
Wilton
Cork

Hardback ISBN: 978-1-84889-220-0
PDF eBook ISBN: 978-1-84889-874-5
EPUB eBook ISBN: 978-1-84889-875-2
Kindle ISBN: 978-1-84889-876-9

Typesetting by Patricia Hope
Typeset in Sabon

Printed in Poland by Drukarnia Skleniarz

CONTENTS

Science is wonderfully equipped to answer the question 'How?' but it gets terribly confused when you ask the question 'Why?'

ERWIN CHARGAFF (1905–2002)

Introduction

Living in the twenty-first century means living at pace with a constant barrage of information and demands from all sides.

I awake and prod young, inert bodies to life, turn on lights, fry eggs, pour calorie-laden cereal, jam lunches into bags, empty smelly gym bags and root around for clean T-shirts and socks, pile everything and everyone into the car and crawl, monosyllabically, to school, college, work; through grey, grey sodden streams of traffic. Where is the sun? Is it still up there hidden behind smog-infested rainclouds? Is the river going to pour over the bank again and seep through sodden sandbags onto kitchen floors, office space and shop fronts? Is the world coming to an end?

Children climb out of cars, slam doors, forget lunches, art work and gym bags as they trudge through the rain to another day as I continue on to the next battle – the workplace.

Sometimes we are so busy and caught up in this frenetic pace, we barely have time to breathe. Often, this can result in confusion and exhaustion. When we do stop we frequently ask 'what is it all for?' Just as often it is difficult to find an answer.

This book attempts to take a look at some of those questions that we ask ourselves from time to time in those grey, traffic-fuelled, hapless moments of existence:

> What is it to be alive in the twenty-first century?
> What is the meaning of life?
> What does it mean to live a useful life?
> What will your legacy be?
> Do you believe in the afterlife and does that affect how you live in this world?

These questions were put to people from varying walks of life, not all well known but all thinkers – writers, poets, philosophers, academics, journalists and teachers, religious and charity workers, and self-proclaimed show-offs, among others.

Here is what they said.

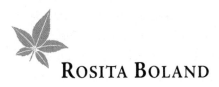

ROSITA BOLAND

I DISTINCTLY RECALL the moment I became aware of the fact of my death at some time in the future, and the visceral shock of that realisation. That moment is the one I identify with the loss of innocence.

It occurred when I was a child, sitting up in bed one night, reading old copies of my mother's *House and Garden* magazine. Then as now, I loved looking at pictures of other people's houses: tiny glimpses of the lives of people I'd never meet. In one photo spread of a country house in rural England, there was a picture of a small child, a girl, about my age, which was eight.

Except she was no longer eight. The magazines were two decades old, and when I did the maths by looking at the date on the front, I realised the 'child' in the photos would be almost thirty.

At some point that evening, I realised two things

simultaneously: that I too would grow older, and that I would die. The magazines I was perusing had been published before I was born. I was in the middle of a cycle of life that would go on no matter what. It was an enormous, terrifying, irreversible knowledge. It still is.

I do not believe in life after death. I believe the actuality of living is all we get, and that it is the responsibility of each of us to treasure every day we have; to not take life for granted; to live as full and fulfilling a life as possible.

Apart from family and friends, which are a given, the things that give meaning to my life are various. Curiosity. Travel. Creativity. Stimulation. Conversation. My job as a reporter. They're the high-minded ones. But some of the happiest ongoing experiences of my life are so simple: walks by the ocean; a glass of champagne with friends; the pleasure of a new *New Yorker* arriving through the letterbox. Living a meaningful life surely doesn't mean everything about it has to be 'meaningful'. That would be both exhausting and unachievable.

There is a wall of graffiti not far from my home in Dublin, on Camden Street, painted by the street artist Maser. In huge white letters on a bright blue background, it states: '*You Are Alive. Avail of this once in a lifetime opportunity.*' I can never pass that wall without promising myself yet again to try and make the most of my life. I don't believe in any kind of god, but I love this urban prayer, and try to live by its direction.

Rosita Boland is a news features writer with The Irish Times, *specialising in human-interest stories. Born in Clare in 1965, she studied at Trinity College Dublin and has published two collections of poetry and two non-fiction travel books:* Sea Legs *(1995, New Island Books) and* A Secret Map of Ireland *(2005, New Island Books). She has travelled extensively and lived in Australia and London as well as Dublin where she now resides.*

Sea Legs *is an account of hitchhiking around the Irish coast.* A Secret Map of Ireland *is an account of a visit to each of the 32 counties on the island and brings back tales so unusual that they could only be 'of Ireland'. She was a 2009 Nieman Fellow at the Nieman Foundation for Journalism at Harvard University.*

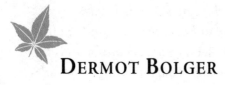

DERMOT BOLGER

Where we are now

(From The Venice Suite: A Voyage Through Loss)

Three years have passed since a day of incessant
  snow
That hailed at midnight, when I ventured with our
  boys
Through the unchained park gates opposite our
  house

Into a white moonscape untainted by footsteps or
  bird claw.
Squadrons of swollen clouds impeded any moon or
  starlight.
Allowing an eerie luminosity to emanate from the
  ground.

Branches overburdened, benches twice their natural
size.
Each everyday object transformed into a source of
light.
The ordinary made wondrous: rendered gleaming
at midnight.

We three raced home to try and lure you from your
bed
To share in our witnessing of this miraculous
spectacle.
But you complained you were sleepy, snuggled
down.

You waved aside each entreaty as we begged you to
come.
'*Not tonight*', you said. '*Not now, but I promise the
next time.*'

None of us could have conceived that when the
snow next fell
It would cover your grave for weeks, leaving us
shell-shocked,
Mutely comforting each other as we mourned your
absent radiance.

Two years after your death, I have finally built our
extension.
With six feet of balustraded decking, five steps
above the garden.

Our sons have converted it into an impromptu
  amphitheatre.

Tonight its recessed lights are abetted by the
  colossal supermoon
That occurs each twenty years, when its orbit is
  nearest the earth.

Guitars and a mandolin have been brought out to
  accompany songs
Composed by your sons and their friends, interspersed
  with old tunes

You would love to hear, as lads pass around long-
  necked foreign beers.
We three have known grief, have carried coffins
  thrice in two years.

But tonight is serenely beautiful: this is where we
  are, in this moment
That cannot be repeated. You'd love to sit here, but
  if you were in bed

I would need to plead and coax you to get dressed
  and wander down.
With you protesting 'Not tonight, not now, but I
  promise the next time.'

Next time a supermoon occurs our sons will be
    forty and forty-one:
I may be a pensioner of seventy-three or be long
    since deceased.

I don't know what or where I will be, I am robbed
    of all certainty,
Liberated from trying to predict the future or shield
    you from it.

I know only the single lesson we have been taught
    by your death:
There is no next time; no moment will replicate the
    wonder of now.

I feel you have moved on and I possess no desire to
    hold you back:
But, just this once, don't say *'Not tonight, but I*
promise the next time.'

Don't argue or prevaricate, but let your ghost come
    and sit unnoticed,
On the wooden steps of this moonlit deck that
    throbs with song.

Be with us, for the eternity of this supermoon, as
    guitars change hands:
See what fine sons you blessed the world with: what
    good friends

They have summoned around them with music and
    chilled beer
Two years on and this is where we are: mourning
    you deeply still.

Yet moving on, as we must move on: our eldest
    finished his degree.
Our youngest immersed in college life, their dad in
    a battered hat.

Joining the gathering briefly to share shots of
    Jägermeister

We don't know where you are, but we are finding
    ourselves again.
I don't know if ghosts exist or just a welcoming
    emptiness awaits.

All I know is that, if you were here, dragged
    protesting from bed,
You would love to hear these songs, these subtle
    guitar riffs.

So, whether your ghost sits here or not, I want you
    to know we are okay
As I call you back to be with us one last time and
    then let you depart.

Born in Dublin in 1959, the poet, playwright and novelist Dermot Bolger has also worked as a factory hand, library assistant and publisher. At the age of eighteen, he established the Raven Arts Press which was one of Ireland's most innovative publishing houses, releasing debut poetry collections by Sara Berkeley, Rosita Boland and Richard Kearney; first books by Colm Tóibín, Fintan O'Toole and Kathryn Holmquist and also major books by Sebastian Barry, Anthony Cronin and Paul Durcan. In 1992 Bolger closed down Raven Arts Press and was involved in co-founding New Island. Bolger's ten novels include The Journey Home, The Family on Paradise Pier *and* The Fall of Ireland. *His plays include* The Ballymun Trilogy *and a stage adaptation of Joyce's* Ulysses. *Bolger writes for most leading Irish newspapers and in 2012 was named Commentator of the Year at the Irish Newspaper Awards. In 2012, his poem sequence,* The Venice Suite: A Voyage through Loss, *in which he commemorated his late wife Bernie, was published by New Island who published his* Selected Poems *in autumn 2014.*

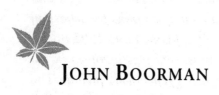

JOHN BOORMAN

FOR MOST OF us the search for meaning is overtaken by the distractions of getting and spending, of love and strife or the urgent needs of an empty stomach.

When we have a spare moment we might consider the painter who wrestles meaning from colour and shape and form. S/he offers us messages torn from chaos. We stare at the paintings in the gallery where they are framed and lit to convince us of their relevance. We are hungry for meaning, we want to believe, but are these profound signals or meaningless daubs?

Mathematics imposes order on matter, but at the sub-atomic level, it is confounded by perverse contradictions.

A soaring Mahler symphony can persuade us that it is divinely inspired, yet why would such a god be, in all other respects, so malignant? Or is it the other way round? Is Mahler trying to compose a god? Is it all upside down?

Instead of God creating the universe, is evolution's aim to create a god?

I have spent my life making movies, an enterprise that involves many skills, much technology and money. The huge effort involved is out of all proportion to the modest result – insubstantial images flickering on a wall or on a smartphone – yet we strive and strain every sinew to achieve them. We must, for we are creating a parallel world that is replete with the meaning missing from life.

I live among trees. They are silent and indifferent yet they comfort me, root me in this valley of Wicklow. As I walk among them, they remind me that I am passing through, a temporary intruder, of little moment.

Would I have missed this spectacle? Not for the world.

John Boorman is a film director, screenwriter, author and playwright. His films include: Point Blank, Deliverance, Excalibur, Hope and Glory, Emerald Forest, The General. *He is currently editing a new film,* Queen and Country. *He claims to have cast Nicol Williamson and Helen Mirren as Merlin and Morgana respectively, against both their protests, in* Excalibur *(1981) because he thought their real-life dislike for each other would give their scenes more of an edge. When sent an early draft of a script for* Rocky *(1976) by producer Robert Chartoff, he allegedly wrote back to say that he was not only not interested but that he strongly advised Chartoff to drop the project completely.*

He lives in a Georgian rectory in County Wicklow.

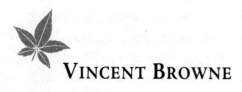

VINCENT BROWNE

Q: What gives meaning to your life?

A: Arguing for/promoting the idea of equality – equality of respect, of income and wealth, equality of access to health and education resources. I have come to believe that absolute equality of income and wealth is essential for differentials in income and wealth gives rise, unavoidably, to inequalities in other spheres.

Q: What does it mean to live a useful life?

A: Promotion of the ideals of equality and justice and kindness to people, with whom we live, work and commune.

Q: What will your legacy be when you are gone?

A: The idea of leaving a legacy is a conceit.

Q: Do you believe in a life after death and does that influence the way you live in this world?

A: I do not believe in a life after death. Yes, that does influence me in that I believe that the promotion of justice is a here-and-now project – a belief in an afterlife allows the deferment of that.

Vincent Browne, originally from Broadford, County Limerick, began his journalistic career by reporting for The Irish Times *from Prague from August to November 1968 on the Soviet invasion of Czechoslovakia. From 1970 to 1994 he worked for numerous magazines and newspapers, including* The Irish Press *and* Sunday Independent. *In 1977 he founded* Magill *magazine, which he edited until 1983. He was subsequently editor of* The Sunday Tribune *(1983–1994), joining* The Irish Times *as a columnist in 1994. He presented* Tonight with Vincent Browne *for RTÉ (1996–2007) and for TV3 since 2007.*

JOAN BURTON

I'VE ALWAYS BELIEVED that one of the most important things in life is to look continuously for the good in people, to see life as a gift and remain hopeful and optimistic even in very difficult situations. But there are times, of course, when mention of the words hope and optimism seems mocking, because of the sheer scale of despair and suffering a people or a country has endured.

When I was Minister for Development Cooperation and Overseas Aid in the 1990s, I made a number of visits to Rwanda in the aftermath of the 1994 genocide. An estimated 800,000 men, women and children – or three-quarters of the minority Tutsi population – were wiped out by the majority Hutu regime's militias. Moderate Hutus were also murdered. On one of the visits, we saw bones sticking out of the ground. It is a memory that will never leave me. In that mind-numbing period, basic principles of human life – that we treat others as our equals – were abandoned in favour of mass murder.

The West failed when it came to Rwanda. It was why I subsequently suggested, as Minister, that the international community had to put in place specific conflict-prevention strategies as part of their overseas development aid policies. Conflict prevention is an essential part of life, from the level of the family to the most powerful nation state.

We cannot place too high a value on dialogue – the simple act of talking. Dialogue underpins the European project. The EU is understandably not a popular concept in Ireland right now, because as an institution it was lacking in its response to the 2008 financial crash, with major consequences for this country. But it should not be forgotten that at the heart of the European project was the desire to move the continent away from war. The significance of that tectonic shift, and the decades of peace that followed, is sometimes lost.

The 1950 Schuman Declaration – the start of the process of European integration – stated that: 'The contribution which an organised and living Europe can bring to civilisation is indispensable to the maintenance of peaceful relations.' Dialogue became the way of European life, and even when the outcomes achieved through diplomacy seem imperfect or incomplete, they ensure that we do not resort to violence.

Mandela said no one was born hating another person – that 'people must learn to hate, and if they can learn to hate, they can be taught to love, for love comes more naturally to the human heart than its opposite'. He counselled against vengeance, because, as he would later tell the Oireachtas in 1990 following his release from prison, 'We understood that to emulate the barbarity of the tyrant would also transform us into savages . . . We had to refuse that our long sacrifice should make a stone of our hearts.' Throughout his long fight, even when the abhorrent apartheid system was at its height and seemed indestructible, he remained hopeful and optimistic. 'It always seems impossible until it's done,' he said.

It's a motto I believe we can all hold close to our hearts.

Joan Burton was appointed Minister for Social Protection in March 2011 and became Tánaiste and Leader of the Labour Party in July 2014. She was the first TD to be re-elected in the general election after topping the poll in Dublin West. Her main priority is to transform the system of social protection to encourage unemployed people back to work, education or training.

One of her key initiatives is the launch of JobBridge, an internship programme, which enables the unemployed to obtain quality work experience. She has also launched a major crackdown on fraud to ensure that the resources of her department are spent on the people who most need them.

CLAIRE BYRNE

FOR ME, BEING alive in the world is a very different prospect from what it meant a year ago: giving birth to my first child has changed my life profoundly.

Patrick has altered how I see the world. He has made me more empathetic and I think I operate differently both at work and in my private life. There is no end to the worry and the guilt and the busyness – but all of that is compensated for when that giggle comes first thing in the morning or a new developmental milestone is reached and I feel like I have won gold at the Olympics. Having Patrick has given me a new understanding of the difficulties that people face in their lives. Now my blood runs cold at the thought of having a sick child; I cannot even contemplate how one survives the death of a child. This deeper understanding is all new to me.

Up until now, the real meaning in my life came from

my work and I am lucky enough to do something that I really enjoy. It has been very healthy for me to have a new focus because almost all of my energy would previously have been devoted to my work and striving to do as much as possible, as well as possible, all of the time. Now I have learned to prioritise and do what I do as well as I can, but perhaps not devote my entire being to my work. This has been beneficial to the quality of my output and also my own quality of life.

I never contemplate not living a useful life – although that phrase is certainly open to interpretation! For me, I have always wanted to achieve and be the best at whatever I turn my hand to. It has not always worked, though, and there have been times when I have realised that I was never going to be the best and those projects or attempts to learn skills are dropped like a hot potato. It is why I never pursued music or art – I knew that I would never excel in those areas, so they wouldn't give me the pleasure that mastering something does. It is also probably why I haven't many hobbies – unless I can be really good at something, I'm not interested.

I don't really believe in leaving a legacy. It would be nice to be remembered for something – but I won't be here, so why would I care? As long as my son and my family think well of me both when I am here and after I am gone, that will be good enough for me. I don't think medals and attributes are very important – you still have to get up and do what you do the next day and the day after.

Being alive now is very exciting for me. After twenty

years of being an adult in the world, I have reached a new and wonderful phase.

Claire Byrne is a broadcaster with RTÉ. She currently presents the current affairs TV show Prime Time, *the radio programme* Morning Ireland *and the political panel show* Saturday with Claire Byrne.

Claire, who is from Laois, has worked as a journalist and presenter in London, Dublin and the Channel Islands for the past twenty years.

'Your living is determined not so much by what life brings to you as by the attitude you bring to life; not so much by what happens to you as by the way your mind looks at what happens'

KHALIL GIBRAN (1883–1931)

NOELLE CAMPBELL-SHARP

AS IT HAPPENS I am here on a train from Killarney to Dublin, a journey I often take between the two centres of my little universe – my art gallery now located opposite the United Arts Club (founded by William Butler Yeats and friends) in Upper Fitzwilliam Street in Dublin 2 and my home in Ballinskelligs near my beloved Cill Rialaig Project, the artist retreat I founded together with my friends in 1991.

The ruins of the pre-Famine village on Bolus Head haunted me for months after first seeing it whilst studying its magnificent stonework with my friend, architect Alfred Cochrane, who had been tasked with the restoration of some similarly-dated ruined buildings nearby, which I wanted as a personal country retreat far from the cruel world of publishing.

And when I heard about its most famous inhabitant, the seanchaí (storyteller) Seán Ó Connaill, and read his colourful stories, it seemed he was calling me back to save his old village from the threat of the Celtic Tiger – an animal that had already stretched its greedy claws to serene southwest Kerry.

There were people who wanted the village ruins demolished to make way for another 'ring road' to take the big tour buses through Ballinskelligs and up the winding sky road of Bolus Head up the cul de sac (a walkers' paradise) to view the Skelligs and the Blasket Islands before carrying on via a new road over Ducalla.

I could see the phenomenal destruction of this rare and precious boreen with its pre-Famine husbandry still evident in the beautiful stone walls, the potato ridges in patchwork fields, still telling its long history to all who walked there, the ancient monastic site with its cross stone slabs and souterrain innocently inviting trouble from the hordes of momentary visitors. Seán cried out to me, it seemed . . . Do something.

So I thought if I found my stone house overlooking Ballinskelligs Bay with the islands of Scariff and Deenish poised perfectly below to be the ultimate 'retreat' then so might it be for others! For other 'storytellers' like Sean since I had always believed all art to be just that – storytelling. The idea came to me to buy the old ruins and rebuild Sean's village using traditional materials of stone and thatch, find a way of letting light through the little cow byres at the back of the houses and then invite the kind of people who would appreciate the real value of this extraordinary place – artists, writers, composers from not only all counties in Ireland but from all over the world.

And to offer a non-commercial ethos – a no-strings-attached sanctuary for the weary artist, blocked writer, retreats of one to four weeks where creativity could blossom – but by invitation only – excellence and need being the two defining elements to our arts organisation's professional selection. A cautious Arts Council Grant of £10,000 gave us hope that despite our very remote situation other enlightened powers that be in Dublin might hear our voice and 'see' the vision.

I was lucky to find not only those business friends in my past who would become patrons and help us rebuild the village but also a wonderful group of local people heartened that their beautiful Bolus Head could be saved and a whole new concerned visitor group identified who would enjoy short residencies throughout the year and bring new life to the area. What they could not have imagined is the way in which those visiting artists from abroad would become cultural ambassadors all over the country and the world itself – telling stories inspired by Seán's deserted village, now a hive of artistic productivity leading to the Cill Rialaig Arts Centre in Dun Geagan, Ballinskelligs, a print studio, ceramic workshop and a flowering of latent local artistic talent. It was all there in the little economically and politically forgotten population.

That's *why I am* still *here*!

Noelle Campbell-Sharp was born in Dublin in 1943 and was adopted by the Roche family of Wexford. She left

school at fifteen, but won critical acclaim with the Young Dublin Players, which led to a position as Public Relations Official for the Gaiety Theatre. Subsequently she became owner and publisher of Irish Tatler Publications.

After the loss of her shares during the Maxwell Communications collapse, Noelle moved to Ballinskelligs in Kerry where she and several friends founded the Cill Rialaig Project, an endeavour to restore a pre-Famine village and create a new artistic and community retreat. She is also owner of the Origin Gallery in Dublin and has served on the Arts Council.

Patricia Casey

THE TWENTY-FIRST CENTURY is a time of contradiction. It is both hugely exciting but enormously daunting. The excitement lies in our ready access to information. Those now in their seventies can barely grasp the momentous spread of information that the Internet allows – ranging from simple news and even gossip to scientific information of a most complex and unimaginable kind. For many professionals, such as doctors, scientists and historians, keeping up with the output in our own area of expertise has become an unachievable feat. Increasingly, tools are being devised to assist us in identifying the most relevant material but in themselves these are also complex and demand focus and precision when we use them. The dangers of psychological overload are ever-present. And the speed of communication, especially using email, is so great that answers are demanded almost immediately, leaving little time for careful deliberation and processing. It forces us to live in the here and now and eschew longer-term considerations. Quelling the demand for immediate answers is a continuing challenge that few can withstand.

Social media, such as Twitter, Facebook and YouTube, have added an altogether new dimension to our style of communication and its impact. They have become so influential that they are said to have played a significant role in the election of Barack Obama as president of the US and in stimulating the Arab Spring, events that led to the fall of totalitarian regimes in that part of the world. These effects are explained by the massive and rapid reach of information to the public. But rapid dissemination of news can also be counterproductive and may facilitate the speedy crushing of peaceful protest. Instant communication in this manner facilitates dictators and idealists alike. Faced with a disinterested or even hostile media in respect of certain social issues, those of us who engage with the public on these reap some benefits from the new social media as they allow voices to be heard that would otherwise be silenced

But as well as exhilaration, the twenty-first century is daunting, not least because of the very worrying underbelly to the social media. Under cover of anonymity, individuals are free to launch *ad hominem* attacks and throw personal insults towards those with whom they disagree in a manner that would not occur in the traditional media. Indeed, it is difficult not to believe that there is a deep volcano of anger that erupts uncontrollably in response to relatively minor disagreements. At times this crosses over into cyberbullying and cyberstalking, phenomena unheard of a decade ago. Other major concerns exist about new cyber behaviours such as sexting, grooming and cyber-sex, which encompass crime and deep psychological dysfunction.

A further challenge is the manner in which new technologies have, over the past decade, irrevocably changed the way in which we live as families. Many of us remember sitting at home glued to our TV sets as the first man walked on the moon or when the Berlin Wall fell. There was a sense that if we did not witness these momentous events they would be lost forever. The family gathered around the television set to capture a once-in-a-lifetime occurrence is now a thing of the past, with playback and retrieval facilities now part of our everyday viewing habits. If families no longer eat together, they also do not watch television together, and so they are becoming fragmented by new technologies. Has this resulted in a loss of our sense of awe and wonder? If we do not engage in major events in real time there is a real chance they will have lost their emotional impact by the time we press our playback button. They are history by then and any personal meaning they might have will have been distilled and dissipated. So asking the question 'Where were you when President Kennedy died?' may no longer have any resonance in the future when the great moments in our history are contemplated.

But despite the volume of information available to us and the speed of everyday life, human beings still have the same innate needs. We need to be born, ideally, into stable families and shown consistent love and nurturing. We need to be given structure in our lives and to be moderate in our habits. We need to have goals and aspirations to enrich us in our journey. And we all need to show love to others as well as being recipients. It is these personal and social bonds which sustain us. If any of these are missing we run the risk of emotional instability and personal discontentment. Above all, we need the physical contact of another human being, to hug, to hold, to touch. As one lonely mother whose son had emigrated remarked, 'I can't hug him on Skype.' No, indeed!

Patricia Casey is Professor of Psychiatry at University College Dublin and Consultant in the Mater Hospital, Dublin. She is the author of ten books and has contributed chapters to twenty-six others. A regular contributor to the media, mainly on social issues and on psychiatry, she also writes a weekly column ('Mind and Meaning') for the Irish Independent.

Patricia is co-founder and patron of the Iona Institute, a Catholic think tank.

GERARD CASEY

A WOULD-BE STUDENT comes to the Philosophy stand at the University's open day and asks the philosopher sitting at the table, 'What's Philosophy?' He replies, somewhat uncomfortably (philosophers hate this question!), 'Well, it's the discipline that asks questions such as "Who am I?", "Where have I come from?", "Why am I here?" – that's Philosophy.' The student looks quizzically at our philosopher and remarks, 'Philosophy? Sounds more like amnesia to me!'

Many a true word is spoken in jest. Philosophy often comes across as an activity conducted by intellectually high-grade and expensively trained amnesiacs. How can philosophers ask such embarrassing questions with a straight face?

Because the answers we give to these questions are what gives meaning to our lives.

Most of us, most of the time, are fully seized by the concerns of the moment. We find ourselves pitched into a busy and demanding world. There's that already-late report to complete, a school run to make, a doctor's appointment to keep, next month's conference to plan for. Who's got time to think? Who's got time to ask the ridiculous questions that philosophers ask?

All of us.

The only way to keep these questions at bay is to keep busy, busy, busy. But life has a way of forcing these questions on us, sometimes in those quiet moments when we find ourselves alone, face to face with ourselves, with nothing to distract us. Sometimes, more drastically, these questions force themselves upon us in the crisis situations of serious illness or death.

These crises force us to confront the meaning of our lives. You never feel so alive as when you have just escaped death. Imagine getting up on a Monday morning, having the same boring breakfast you always have, going to do the same boring work in the same boring place you've worked for the last boring fifteen years. At work, you collapse and are taken to hospital. They run some tests on you and inform you that you are in the advanced stages of pancreatic cancer and have two months to live. Later that afternoon, an embarrassed house doctor comes back to tell you that the hospital confused your records with those of another patient with the same name and that there is nothing really wrong with you that eating a regular breakfast and getting some exercise won't cure. How do you feel? As if reprieved at the last minute from the firing squad. How does the world look to you now? Alive and vibrant.

Do I believe in life after death? Yes. But I also believe in life before death. I believe in a life in which death is a singular transitional event, a life whose every moment should be a chromatic triumph over grey everydayness. The meaning of my life, its value, is given by my relationships to other people, to my friends, my family and my God and by my work in philosophy. My legacy will be my children and, if I'm very lucky, my writing.

Gerard Casey is a Professor in the School of Philosophy at University College Dublin, Adjunct Professor at the Maryvale Institute (Birmingham, UK) and Adjunct Scholar at the Ludwig von Mises Institute (Auburn, Alabama, USA). His latest book is Murray Rothbard *(Vol. 15 in the series* Major Conservative and Libertarian Thinkers*) which came out in May 2010 (Continuum).*

EOIN CASSIDY

In the Winner's Enclosure

WINNER, ALL RIGHT: in the winner's enclosure you won't find Richard, or Dick, as he was known to his friends. In the capitalist and celebrity culture, which increasingly shapes the Ireland of today, Dick suffered twice. He had already known – nearly all of his life – poverty of spirit: the depression, lack of self-confidence and loss of self-esteem that accompanied him on most days. However, by the late autumn of 2008, in the wake of the precipitous collapse in the value of Irish bank shares, for the first time in his life he was about to become acquainted with the real thing – poverty itself, or at least he would have, if he had not taken matters into his own hands, and taken his own life.

'November 6th 2008: death by misadventure.' I never thought that this phrase did justice to my friend Dick who was said to have been found hanging from a beam in the garden shed, with the briefest of notes carefully folded, as one might fold a handkerchief, and placed in the top pocket of his best suit jacket. It simply read, 'My Dearest Pat, terribly sorry that I could no longer provide for you. Love, Dick.'

Five years on, his anniversary passes once more – 6 November – the feast of all the Irish Saints. I find myself wondering whether there are any saints left today – if there are any 'blessed' people in a new post-bailout Ireland, just what would they look like. Having been left to pick up the pieces of financial ruin all by herself, Pat was in no humour to see anything funny about the outrageous idea of her husband being nominated as 'blessed' Dick. Furthermore, by her reckoning, his suicide was the ultimate betrayal – the act of a coward. Needless to say, there were no cowards in her list of saints or blessed people in a modern secular Ireland. Imagining herself to be a type of spiritual Dragon on *Dragons' Den*, she advocated the no-nonsense culture of what she described as 'Entrepreneurs for Christ'. The way that she sees it, Ireland would be a much richer land in every sense if we encouraged a straight-talking culture of risk-takers who would promote Gospel values.

Although the title 'Entrepreneurs for Christ' may have an odd ring to it, nevertheless there are few who would question the validity of risk-taking with a view to promoting Gospel values. Problems emerge, however, in the way in which an emphasis on risk-taking and entrepreneurship reinforces the capitalist cultural mores of the increasingly competitive and celebrity-obsessed culture in Ireland today. Such an environment was directly responsible for the rise of a culture of entitlement which, with top-up payments and bonuses, was directly responsible for the excesses of the Celtic Tiger and which even today continues to engender anger across all segments of Irish society. Finally, it should not be forgotten that it effectively divides the world into winners and losers, and as Dick's suicide reminds us, in extreme circumstances, it can drive those so-called losers over the edge of the precipice.

Imagine a world in which there are no losers. Even John Lennon's 1972 iconic anthem for a better world did not contain such a 'foolishly' utopian ideal. And yet, is it so foolish? What about that extraordinary inversion of values in the founder of Christianity's proclamation of a loser's charter, *Blessed are the poor in spirit . . . Blessed are the poor . . .* Could we imagine an Ireland in which there are no losers but only winners, a country in which one could stand shoulder to shoulder with the likes of Dick and help him to acknowledge his own blessedness? This scenario is about as realistic as imagining omnipotence transformed mysteriously into impotence, or indeed, an all-powerful God, mocked, ridiculed, and finally dying on a cross, with only four people, including his mother, who would make it to his funeral. To cut a long story short, this suggests that there is very little danger of a cultural change that would allow life's losers into the winner's enclosure. Or perhaps not: one never knows. Winner, all right?

46

Eoin G. Cassidy is a priest of the Dublin diocese and head of the Philosophy department at Mater Dei Institute of Education, Dublin City University. He is a former executive secretary of the Irish Centre for Faith and Culture and for the past six years has worked as a member of the Irish Commission for Justice and Peace. He has published widely in these and other related areas.

VICTORIA MARY CLARKE

I HAVE ABSOLUTELY no idea why I am here.

Indeed, I am never entirely certain that I am here at all.

For when I dream at night I am quite convinced that the dream is where I am.

So it may well be that this too is a dream from which I will awaken and think 'Now I shall get on with my real life'.

But if I were really here, and there were a reason to be here, what might that reason be?

Might it be so that I can meet the people who are also here?

Can there be anything in this existence more thrilling than the feeling of love that we are capable of sharing?

If I were told that tomorrow I would no longer 'be here', unless I could argue convincingly to be allowed to stay, what would I say?

I would say that I want to be here because there is so much to enjoy about being here, there is a feeling that happens in my heart so much of the time, a feeling like my heart is doing a dance of joy.

Not everything about this life excites me or brings me joy, it is important to say. There are things that make me sad, things that make me fearful, dreadful things. The pain and suffering that we witness here is as excruciating as the good stuff is delightful. But the good stuff is truly delightful.

Some people say that we have come here to learn lessons.

I don't know if that is true.

If I have learned any lesson it is that there is always another surprise waiting, something that you did not expect. Life is far, far stranger than you ever dream it will be.

There is also a notion that we are here to contribute something, that our souls have assigned us a 'mission'.

If I have a mission, I hope that it is to explore as much as possible of this life and the possibilities that it holds. I see my own life as having been a voyage of discovery.

And if I were to contribute something, I would hope to contribute the benefits of my own discoveries, so that other people might enjoy the things that I have enjoyed. Sort of like a *Lonely Planet* guide to living. I don't know what lies beyond this reality that we call 'life'. But I have experienced many sensational adventures that seemed to involve unseen beings. I have spent a great deal of time conversing with non-physical beings that I call angels. One of my adventures involved learning to 'channel' light beings, guides and angels. I talk to them a lot, and these conversations have given me some of the most blissful and profound experiences of my life so far. It is during these communications that I truly feel that whatever this life is all about, however long it is and whatever lies in store for me, it is entirely perfect and completely safe and nothing at all to worry about!

Victoria Mary Clarke is an Irish human/writer/journalist/ broadcaster/yoga teacher/angel channeller/explorer/and co-founder of Speaking Suppers (among other things). She lives in Dublin with her partner Shane MacGowan and grows tomatoes.

EVELYN CONLON

I HAVE, OF course, been resisting writing answers to the question of what it is to be alive at all, never mind the year, because it can be a very dangerous thing to think about, dangerous to stop and actually answer, rather than rush, or even joyously muddle, through the week with several lists, two diaries, personal notes, reams of paper, a telephone, a Leap Card and some drugs, tea and the like. The effort of replying brings to mind one of the few science fiction type books I ever read. The women go on strike and send the children to work with the men. A child asks her busy production-line father what he is doing and why. It's a voice he's used to answering so he stops and says 'What?', and suddenly there's all hell to pay. Being alive in this time is probably no different from being alive in others, except for the noise of self-importance. That's a bit loud these days.

Meaning comes from decency, knowing that there are people who haven't sold their souls, who live for what is right and not for what they can covertly gain for themselves. It comes from knowing that there are still people who would say 'You first', at the lip of the lifeboat. It comes from having a book of poems and some meaningful fiction open on the table. To live a useful life means to spend time being other than simply on the lookout for oneself. To have conversations that raise themselves higher than gossip. Luck is to have friends to do that with. And to write stories, of course, ones that may mean exactly what they appear to mean, or may not. It is easy to be vague about what fiction is if you have walked on Death Row.

My legacy when I'm gone? That's easy: it will presumably be my own books and the way I looked at the work of others. It will, of course, also be those young men who were and are actually my children – I still have no idea how that happened – and their children and, who knows, maybe their children. I almost forgot the crèche in Maynooth. But if none of all that had happened, would that mean that I had no legacy? Surely not.

I spent a good part of my early life getting rid of the notion of life after death. I think dealing with this one is enough to be going on with. If there is something after, I hope it's as good and not as bad as this one. The notion of heaven and hell, as drummed into us as children, always seemed too complicated to me, too much of a lottery about it for this supposedly worked-out God. What if you'd been a really good person and committed only one sin in your life but got killed by the ceiling falling in as you waited to go to confession? How could that mean that you were going to hell, when the person who had sinned all his life but just happened to have come out of the box got hit by the same beam? By the time I was ten I felt that was a non-runner. And as I got older and thought of the people who were supposedly going to hell I realised that I liked them better. It's an interesting thing to become an atheist, though, because one has to live by moral standards as opposed to religious laws. You have to think out more things. So yes, in answer to the question about the effect of belief/non-belief, I think that not believing in a god, and certainly rearing children without the threatening presence of one, meant that a lot of time was spent thinking about what was the right thing to do.

Evelyn Conlon is a novelist and short story writer. Born in County Monaghan, she lives in Dublin and has a deep interest in Australia where she lived in the early 1970s, having set off on an adventure to the bottom of the world at the age of nineteen.

Returning to Ireland in 1975, she had a child and started an undergraduate degree in Maynooth. After the birth of her second child, she separated from the children's father.

A stint in teaching ended abruptly when she was peremptorily dismissed; her 'separated status' and identification with the Irish Women's Liberation movement were not appreciated. At this point she decided to become a freelance writer to keep the wolf from the door. However, it was not until her children entered their teenage years that her writing really began to take off.

Her novel, Skin of Dreams *(2003, Brandon/Mount Eagle), shortlisted for Irish Novel of the Year, examines capital punishment and her research included a visit to death row in the US to help her understand her own position.*

Her most recent novel, Not the Same Sky *(2013, Wakefield Press) draws on her Australian experience, a place that she has become besotted by; the landscapes, the colour, the wildlife as well as the people.*

'Go *confidently in the direction* of *your dreams. Live the life you have imagined.*'

HENRY DAVID THOREAU (1817–1862)

MAEVE COOKE

In 2001 MY German mother-in-law died quite suddenly at the age of seventy-eight. We had got along very well until ten years previously, when her son, an only child, gave up a promising career as a teacher in Germany to be a husband in Dublin. She took some time to adjust. The birth of our daughter in 1996 helped considerably and she became a wonderful grandmother. She visited us regularly in Ireland and welcomed us into her life in Germany whenever we were there. My relationship with her regained much of its former warmth and easiness and developed in scope and depth. She loved Ireland and my Irish family, who returned her affection. Nonetheless, I felt that she never completely accepted her son's alternative life path in a country almost a thousand miles away from her. I understood the difficulties and empathised. However, her residual sadness cast a shadow over us and I did not expect to react as I did when she died. I felt bereft: deprived of something that lent value to my life. For months afterwards I heard her voice talking to me in the kitchen (though we had rarely cooked together), I felt her presence at work (where she had never accompanied me), I saw her watching our daughter reading storybooks (who could not yet read while she was alive). In brief, after her death her spirit lived on for me in an immediate, embodied way. While I have come to believe in this kind of life after death, traditional Christian views on the resurrection of the body do not speak to me; the same is true of many other religious views on reincarnation.

Although I do not hold any orthodox religious belief in life after death, I do not view life as meaningless. On the contrary, my days are full to overflowing with activities that I perceive as important, mainly (though not only) because I see them as contributing to the well-being of other people, directly or indirectly. Yet I do not find life easy. I had a privileged upbringing, not financially but in almost every other respect, and this privilege has continued in adulthood. There is almost no area – family, work, health, money – where I am not better off than most people. This is not just from the outside looking in: I experience myself as extremely privileged, am deeply appreciative of my good fortune and my sense of it motivates my efforts to help other people wherever I can. This makes it hard to explain why I often feel so burdened by life. But one of the lessons I have learned along the way is not to seek an explanation. An inveterate reader, I find pleasure in the imaginary worlds I frequent; on dark days they are a refuge and source of solace. I have also learned the importance of maintaining good physical habits, good interpersonal habits and good working habits, a corset holding me together on darker days. And I have learned that even the darkest days may have moments of illumination, reminding me of the power of love and the excitement of intellectual ideas.

Maeve Cooke is Professor of Philosophy at University College Dublin and a member of the Royal Irish Academy. She has published widely in the area of social and political philosophy and held visiting appointments at prestigious universities in the USA and Europe. She lives in Dublin.

LUCINDA CREIGHTON

Why am I here?

IN 1989 A famous photograph captured a Chinese man standing alone, dressed in a white shirt and with a grocery bag in hand. He is stopped in the centre of the road to face a foreboding string of military tanks lined up perfectly, one behind the other. This image of the Tank Man epitomises the idea of conscientious objection, and the enormous challenge it is to stand against the odds.

While the man's immediate situation is unique, opportunity for conscientious objection is not. Most of us will never face Panzer tanks or military force. Still, the photograph illustrates the magnitude of the forces we face, both as individuals as well as a society. Forces which are at times contrary to personal beliefs. We are continually confronted with social, economic and political expectations that actively influence our daily choices. These pressures often dictate our decisions and can at times overrule personal values. However, in every situation where a choice is to be made, there is also an opportunity to consciously and confidently take a stand against those conflicting values.

This island has a long history of going against the grain. In fact, our democracy is built on notions of conscientious objection. Parliamentarians therefore have a particular obligation to express authentic, original and quality concerns which reflect the diversity and overarching interests of the people. This is played out daily in the Oireachtas. Every vote is an act on values and beliefs.

However, there is an increased temptation to compromise values in the name of progress: progress which has been defined as moving forward by means of adding, or going further. But at times is it arguably more progressive, more radical, more effective, to pause and, in some cases, hold back.

Throughout my own political career I have done my best in every situation to uphold the values and beliefs of my constituents and the Irish people more generally. The concerns of my constituents have always been at the forefront of each and every decision I have made inside and outside the Dáil. I have tried to maintain that level of accountability under difficult circumstances. I firmly believe true progress is not achievable without a strong willingness to consciously challenge accepted wisdom. Thus, I have done my utmost to demonstrate that philosophy in my work.

As people we must hold ourselves to the same obligation as those in public office. It is vital for the betterment of our communities, to express unease, consciously and genuinely, in situations of moral and ethical relevance. It is a duty we have to ourselves as a part of our own community, and of a common nation, to consider where each of us may rightly express ourselves. There we can make our own conscientious objection, like the Tank Man, to make an important point.

This is what comprises people of integrity. Images like the Tank Man remind us of the significance of the individual who acts on their conscience and recognises the ability of such actions to empower others. And empowering others is where the real difference is made.

Lucinda Creighton has been a TD for the Dublin South-East constituency since 2007. She served as Minister of State for European Affairs from March 2011 to July 2013. She sits as an Independent TD having been expelled from the Fine Gael parliamentary party when she defied the party whip by voting against the Protection of Life During Pregnancy Bill 2013. In September 2013, she, along with six others, formed the Reform Alliance, described as a loose alliance rather than a political party.

JOHN CROWN

I AM NOW fifty-six years old, and one thing that dawns on me with the passing years is that it is very good indeed to be alive. Over the years I have known so many people who were robbed of the opportunity to live a life as long as the one I have led and it makes you cherish every day you have.

My life derives its meaning from my children, now young adults, and also from my extremely interesting career. I think the question of legacies after we die is wrapped up in many aspects of human vanity. Hopefully, the legacy I will leave will be happy children and grandchildren who live happy, productive lives. My major professional legacy is the patients whose lives I have prolonged and, in some cases, saved. Professionally, I am proud of the Irish Cooperative Oncology Research Group which I co-founded and which has brought clinical cancer research to patients the length and breadth of Ireland. I hope I can still make an impact in developing cancer research in Ireland.

I am agnostic on the question of life after death. I had an intensely religious upbringing but will admit to a great scepticism about it at this stage. I certainly am not an atheist. I have an open mind on the possibility and indeed believe that, for a scientist, agnosticism is always the correct intellectual position on everything. I don't believe my life is primarily lived in preparation for a life after death, although I am sure there are probably some subtle aspects of my religious upbringing that do influence some of the decisions I make.

With regard to whether or not I have influenced anything in my writings and work, I hope I've had some bit of an educational role in highlighting the deficiencies in the health services in general and cancer services in particular. I like to think that I have had some role in putting clinical research on the national agenda.

My favourite quote is:

> *The best lack all conviction, while the worst*
> *Are full of passionate intensity.*
>
> WILLIAM BUTLER YEATS, *'The Second Coming'*

John Crown is a professor and consultant medical oncologist at St Vincent's University Hospital, Dublin. He

has helped established three major cancer research groups in Ireland: the Irish Cooperative Oncology Research Group (ICORG) (1996); the Cancer Clinical Research Trust (CCRT) (1997); and Molecular Therapeutics for Cancer Ireland (2009). The work of all these research groups directly benefits cancer patients in Ireland. Since 2011, John has been an Independent member of Seanad Éireann and is also a frequent contributor to the media and professional meetings on the subject of health policy.

Tom Dalzell

Desire

WHAT IS IT that gives meaning to my life? It is what the French call '*désir*'. We human beings are always looking for something. Our hearts are restless, as Augustine once put it. We're dynamic, always seeking, always searching, and it is that very dynamism that makes our lives meaningful. There is always a tension in us. We want and want. Then we decide that we want something in particular. But as soon as we have chosen something to want, we're not satisfied with it. In fact, we are never satisfied with our choices. We are never satisfied with the particular objects we think we want and we start wanting again. That is what keeps us going. It is what makes our lives purposeful.

What gives meaning to life is not so much the object of our desire, what we desire, but the very act of desiring.

And desire is never satisfied. We never really get what we desire. In fact, what we are really looking for keeps receding, keeps moving further away from us. It sounds paradoxical, but if we ever found it, maybe our lives would lose their meaning altogether. If I am here today it is because, thankfully, I still haven't found what I'm looking for. Despite this, the new cultural commandment today is not 'desire!', but 'thou shalt enjoy thyself'. We all know this from our everyday experience. Even in the restaurant, when the meal is served, the waiter or the waitress will say: 'Enjoy!' But is it enjoyment, what the French call *'jouissance'*, that makes our lives meaningful? It is true that we live our lives between desire and enjoyment, limited enjoyment, that is, not too much. But, ultimately, life is not about enjoyment; it is not about attaining what we desire, but simply desiring. That is what gets us up in the morning and gives us something to hope for. It makes our lives worth living. Too much enjoyment, on the other hand, is unbearable. It causes suffering. In fact, getting the object of our desire would be a living death, not life.

Our desire originates because of lack. We have lost something, our first object, and we want to find it again. Having direct access again to paradise lost would put an end to our desire. It would mean the loss of a loss, the lack of a lack, and we would have nothing left to desire. We would have nothing to live for and our lives would be without meaning. Is there any hope for someone who has lost their desire? To my mind, there is always hope for all of us. What was it that caused our desire in the first place?

It was when language came between us and our first object that our desire started. From then on, there was something missing. It is not being separated physically from our mothers that causes desire, but language. It is language that causes the lack that causes desire. And what gives me hope is that we can always speak. Speaking can put an end to enjoyment and replace it with desire. In that way, our lives can find meaning again.

Dr Tom Dalzell is a Lacanian psychoanalyst. He is a lecturer at All Hallows College in Dublin and in the School of Psychotherapy at St Vincent's University Hospital, Dublin. His most recent book is Freud's Schreber *between Psychiatry and Psychoanalysis (2011, Karnac).*

GERALD DAWE

I HAD KNOWN her all my life and when she died it felt that not only had she gone but that her death stood for more than an individual death. For someone so private there was a contradiction to begin with as people stopped me in the street where she had lived her later years – from the mid-1970s to the turn of the new century. They said how sorry they were to hear of her passing. A tearful neighbour recounted how shocked she was by her own reaction on hearing of her death. 'She was such a spiritual woman. She always said something that'd make you think.' 'She was very private too'. And, of course, she was both: in her own way, writing letters to her family, telephoning, sending little cards and presents now and again to her grand-children, expressing her opinion about politics until she got switched off by the currency of complaint and recrimin-ation and petulance which she thought was engulfing the airwaves and civic spaces of today. She became more remote from the 'bigger' issues – of post-Troubles Belfast, her native city – and much more preoccupied with the everyday management of her health, and her husband's health and maintaining the apartment they moved to in their final years.

When I think of her I hear her advice, indeed her injunctions, to 'stick to your own guns', not to play a game of fakery – of currying favour. She was critical of pretence in any shape or form. Promoting oneself was anathema and carried the moral risks of losing faith with what one *really* believed in. It was a hard ask but even if it meant being alone, or in a minority, that was her view. Self-belief was an act of faith; a defining of one's self without boasting or boosting.

Celebrity, fame, reputation, these were suspect, passing achievements when placed alongside the much greater and lasting virtue of being respected, no matter by how many or how few. *That* recognition could only be earned through work and it was in the gift of others to give praise, unheralded and honestly. For those who used their abilities in order to achieve anything else, these were, in her book, lesser achievements, falsified by manipulation and, as such, they meant far less, if anything at all, in the long run.

Such values that she held dear were lived in part unconsciously in the way she related to the world. They were not self-regarding or self-righteous or in any way pompous. Since 'blame' was something she disavowed, her values held no one at fault – except when violence was done – but were finely tuned and pervasive and complicated by the life she had known through good times and through bad. She was stoical by nature. Evacuated during the Belfast blitz of the Second World War, she lost her own mother shortly after the break-up of her marriage in the mid-1950s, followed by the death of her beloved father – all at a relatively young age. She raised a family on her own – two children – before the dire times of the Troubles began. Complaint was not for her.

But irreverent laughter and fun with an ability to overcome the obstacles that came her way meant that there was always about the woman – small in demeanour and undeceiving in mind – an interest and curiosity in the world so that when she died in her eighty-fifth year, the stabilising definition of what she stood for seems all the more telling in her absence.

I wrote this poem 'Natural History' – part of a longer sequence – thinking of my mother, and the journey she would take almost every other day, going up 'the road' for the messages. I think of the influences she handed on to her immediate family, of course, but also, in just being, a quiet determined presence, and see her example as crucial in giving meaning to my life and of what it means to live a 'useful' life:

Natural History

Hedges bulge around giant cypresses
where you'd have walked and seen
the sky lightening at the end of the road
and kept on, by the ancient green

vestibule doors, the untouched front
rooms and darkened hallways, to find
yourself not here any more, not at all,
but in the rush fields of a raven's hill.

*Belfast-born Gerald Dawe has published eight collections
of poetry and four volumes of essays as well as editing
various anthologies of poetry and literary criticism. He is
Professor of English and Fellow of Trinity College Dublin
and founder-director of the Oscar Wilde Centre at Trinity
College. He has held visiting professorships at Boston
College and Villanova University.*

GREG DELANTY

To STATE THE obvious first: I don't have a clue why I'm here or any other being or thing is here, whether it is way out in deep space or way deep within microscopic cells. At the same time I am lucky enough to think and feel that poetry is my life, though why it is I don't *exactly* know. I try not to preoccupy myself with the meaning of why I am here, but at the same time keep in mind as much as a human can: 'How abnormal to think it normal to find ourselves / on a spinning ball reeling around a star / at thousands of miles per hour from who knows where / to who knows where, how outlandish.' What is most import-ant to me is that I renew the world in my poetry, so people can see it anew, can 'Behold the normal' with awe. I think the main function of the artist is to renew.

With regard to what it is to be alive in the twenty-first

century, apart from the poems arising out of the regular subject matter of my private life, I am mostly preoccupied with what humans are doing to our planet. A new book called *So Little Time* is just about to come out here in the US and it is centred on how we are destroying the environment. It is established now that there is little time left for so many plants and creatures, including ourselves, if we go on living as we do. Many have already run out of time. We are turning the planet into a place where we cannot live as a species, or if we do manage to survive, we will live in diminished ways. Yet the governments, and the world in general, continue on as if this is not so. In part this is because we cannot bear to dwell on our dire situation, which results in apathy and denial. Phyllis Windle, in her important article 'The Ecology of Grief,' writes about the shock we feel at realising our situation, and suggests ways we can tackle it. Art is one of those ways. Good art works on many powerful levels, one of which can help us come to terms with our emotions and thoughts: our fear, anger, and loss. It is important that we face our situation and suffer it so we can live in the world in a healthier way.

In the introduction to *So Little Time* I write: 'All my own poems included here were written over a period of 25 years. Many have appeared in other collections. They were written while I was writing other poems arising out of whatever was preoccupying me at the time, whether it was my parents, love, marriage, the birth of my son, or baseball. Since I have also always been preoccupied by what is going on in the world, naturally I wrote poems out of my public concerns, though I never think of them as either public or private. Maybe the only thing that makes a poem public is that it is published for the public to read. What is important for the poet is that the poems work as art, that they are not overwhelmed by the artist on the soapbox. It is only when the art issues from what is genuine that the work is truthful and nourishing.

I believe that poetry can make things happen. W. H. Auden's 'poetry makes nothing happen' is often quoted (though somewhat out of context since it is taken from a poem written within months of the Second World War, which is what Auden, it can be argued, is referring to). The quote is from the poem 'In Memory of W. B. Yeats', and must also be responding to Yeats' fear stated in his poem 'Man and the Echo': 'Did that play of mine send out / Certain men the English shot?' In any case, the Auden quote is wrong in the most obvious way as it provided work for the compositors/printers who produced that book with Auden's own poems, which in turn provided money to feed themselves and their families.

A life dedicated to poetry would be empty if it didn't act upon the truth of its beliefs. For me the time for remaining in the ivory tower of academia and the arts, places of knowledge and privilege, is long past. For over thirty years I have been what people call an activist, standing in vigils and demonstrations, and taking part in civil disobedience actions such as being arrested outside the White House demonstrating against the fossil fuel industry. Recently, I gave up my car here and I cycle and use public transport mostly – though it helps that I live in a city that allows me to do this. I say these things factually to indicate that to me art and life are not separate. I think of them as a palindrome. My poems could not issue from a genuine place in me unless I lived a life true to them. This is my way of being alive.

You ask me if I believe in life after death. I have always felt, even as a child, that too much of this world was focused on the next world. I try to ignore thoughts of an afterlife. For me what is wonderful is this life, with all its difficulty. I am, we are, in the Western World generally, among the lucky ones who do not have to suffer starvation, war and unnecessary degradation like millions of people in other parts of the world. The likes of us have a responsibility to also be glad – even happy sometimes – about being alive. If people like me cannot then who can? So, what I am saying is that this life is the only life I know of. I am not interested in the next, nor will I presume there is one, barring the certainty that we dissolve into the physical world when our bodies decompose – and become gourds, potatoes, dung, maggots, magpies, delicious tomatoes, trees, and maybe even roses will grow out of me and spread out through the world into other living things, including into other humans in the future. Perhaps my poems, figuratively and practically, will do this also. I would like that.

The following is a poem from my latest book, *The Greek Anthology, Book XVII*. Hopefully it relates much of what I have been saying here in a better way:

Patient

The snow has melted clean off the mountain.
It's winter still. Yet another indication that Gaia
is in trouble, that things aren't sound.
The rocky mountain top shines
like the bald head of a woman after chemo
who wills herself out of her hospital bed
to take in the trees, the squirrels, the commotion
in town, sip beer in a dive, smile
at the child ogling her shiny head, wishing
it didn't take all this dying to love life.

Greg Delanty's most recent book is The Greek Anthology, Book XVII *(Carcanet Press). His publications include* Collected Poems 1986–2006, The Ship of Birth, The Blind Stitch *(all published by Carcanet) and* The Hellbox *(1998, Oxford University Press). Another recent book which he edited with Michael Matto is* The Word Exchange: Anglo-Saxon Poems in Translation, *(2011, W.W. Norton).*

Greg's papers, up to 2010, have been acquired by The National Library of Ireland. He has won many awards and his poems have been widely anthologised. He lives in Vermont and is Poet in Residence at Saint Michael's College, Vermont. He returns to his home in Derrynane, County Kerry, every year.

'I haven't a clue how my journey will end, but that's alright. When you set out on a journey and night covers the road, that's when you discover the stars.'

NANCY WILLARD (1936–)

BARRY EGAN

'HERE'S SOME WISDOM just for you,' the actor John Hurt once told me over lunch in Dublin. 'You cannot be happy. It is not a state. It is something that you pass by and you have happiness. Like your childhood. You ask anyone about their childhood. You will find most people will say, "Yes, that was quite happy, I quite enjoyed that . . . oh, I hated that. Oohh, that was horrible. Oh, that was wonderful. I loved it when we were on holiday. Ohh, well, I didn't like it when that happened."

'There are moments. Life is made of moments. That's what it is about. We are ephemeral. We are passing through.'

I often look at the old pictures of my parents, the most obvious answer for why I'm here, in their moments. Searching for some sort of meaning, I wonder what they were thinking when the picture was taken. Smiling on a beach in Benidorm. Looking comfortably numb on the back of a donkey in Killarney. Beaming on their honeymoon in London. They were both in their eighties when they died.

I read some of the old books my father read, and look at the bits he underlined or even the pages he folded, looking for clues from my creator. I play the songs on YouTube that my mother used to sing on the stage in Dublin to imagine the words in her head as she sang them.

I have a picture of my mother, barely twenty, singing on stage at the Theatre Royal in Dublin in the mid 1940s. She had amazing eyes. I wonder what was going on behind her eyeballs as she looked out through them.

There are so many things I should have asked them before they died. So many conversations I was too weak or frightened to have. A friend of mine said to use every opportunity to talk to them before they've gone for good. I had time. I just never had the guts to ask them anything important or even tell them I loved them to their faces.

When they died – in 2009 and 2011 – I told them each in a private moment that I loved them, in the house before their bodies were taken out for the last time. There is a profoundly perverse irony that I can say I love you to their dead selves but not to their living selves. (Sometimes I think my life has turned into a Dave Allen sketch from the 1970s produced by Samuel Beckett or Woody Allen.)

And when I go to the grave to 'visit' Mum and Dad, I say a little prayer, then go home and listen to David Bowie sing about 'Time bends, God is dead, the inner-self is made of many personalities.'

I suppose I am secretly fascinated by the idea of God;

and the possibility – however illogical – it brings of maybe seeing my parents again or friends who have died, like some sort of acid trip in a Beatles song. And when I get to this place called Heaven doubtless my father will mortify me in front of everyone, including John Lennon, Elvis Presley and Marilyn Monroe, by turning to my mother and saying: 'Maureen, that fella still hasn't got his shagging hair cut.'

On Christmas Eve while the rest of Ireland was watching *The Wizard of Oz*, I was re-watching for the hundredth time the DVD extras on Ridley Scott's sci-fi film *Prometheus* where scientists go looking in outer space for the origins of life on earth and to see if God or something else is the creator. In particular the bit where David says to The Engineer, a godlike figure: 'This man is here because he does not want to die. He believes you can give him more life.'

Life is meaningless if it is not absurd. My father can live to eighty-two. Yet the lives of young children and babies went out of existence along with my father. Jean Paul Sartre said that hell was other people. But hell is two- and three-year-olds dying of cancer in a children's hospital. What is the meaning of that? It defies all meaning and even logic.

I was in Rwanda in 1994 two weeks after a million people were murdered in a genocide. Where was God in Rwanda? Or Auschwitz fifty-something years before? Or Syria or Iraq or (insert the country of your choosing here) any time recently?

As children, we are taught to reason in a world that

has no actual reason. This statement may not jump out at you in its originality but it is certainly true on many levels.

I think my life would have no 'meaning' if I didn't have a child to leave behind in this world when I died.

If I ever did become a father – and at forty-six I'd need to get my biological groove on soon – I am frankly terrified about what I'd be expected to tell the child, my child, about life. 'You will understand when you are old enough' and, more probably, 'Don't do what I did, son' will have to do in terms of me providing him with any answers on the meaning of life.

I could simply hand him my DVD of *Prometheus*.

Or I could read my imaginary son a quote my own father liked by Robert Frost: 'In three words I can sum up everything I've learned about life: it goes on.'

Or send him a tweet on Twitter.

Or give him John Hurt's phone number and suggest he call him instead.

Let me end by returning to the lunch with Mr Hurt. 'You see, you want answers for you,' he said, almost chastising me. 'There are no answers. There is a great story of the man who sold his house, left his job, and went to find the guru in the Himalayas. After a year of trying to get there, he finally knocked on the door of the monastery and they said: "What do you want?"

'He said: "I have sold everything. I have come over from Ireland. I want to find out the meaning of life."

'They said: "Go back down the mountain and stay there for a year and come back again." He comes back a year later and finally the guru sees him.

'He says to the guru: "I want to know the meaning of life."

'The guru says: "Life is a bowl of cherries."

'The man says: "I have sold everything and you tell me that life is just a bowl of cherries?"

'So the guru says: "All right – life is not a bowl of cherries."

'It's as simple as that, really,' John Hurt said, then got up and left.

❦

Barry Egan is a chief feature writer and columnist for over twenty years at the Sunday Independent. *He also has his own show* In Conversation . . . *on Radio Nova.*

He meditates twice a day, morning and evening. He suggests it helps him to see the good in people and become less judgemental. Although his girlfriend, sister and copy-editor at the Sunday Independent *might disagree, he thinks he is a little less of a 'moody crankypants' because of transcendental meditation.*

Bernadette Flanagan

The Embrace of Solitude

SOLITUDE FOR ME is a quality of personhood that facilitates singularity of purpose, through coming to know one's unique name. This is not just a matter of finding an acceptable and satisfying blend of involvements in life. Instead, solitude is the space where it is possible to discover the very essence of my own being, what is utterly original and uniquely woven into the fabric of my personhood. I am not an *it* to myself or to God, a project to be managed, a performer of tasks. I am a being which the Spirit is seeking to animate from when I wake to when I sleep. There is unity and integration at the heart of life, a silent music that calls each one to dance in its rhythm. Embracing solitude is the intentional creation of a space where we suspend the external music that can so easily set the pace and rhythm of our daily motion and where instead we redirect our attention to the more fundamental score of the Spirit. Leonard Cohen has aptly described this solitary space as a 'Tower', and his lyrics in the song, 'Tower of Song', invite reflection on the importance of commitment to spending time in the tower, 'tied' to its interior landscape, in order to encounter the divine, inalienable core of one's being in the eyes of God.

Solitude for me is more an attitude than an environment: a lived belief in the need for regular withdrawal to the inner room of my being. Time spent in that inner monastery of being allows what has become muddied and confused in daily living to settle and become clear. In the spirit of Cohen's song, God is calling me from within, to come home to the unique desire that has been placed in my heart by God. I seek to learn the mystery of God's desiring in my heart, the truth of my life and being. Only in solitude can the music to which I am called to dance be heard. It is not effort and striving that makes me as a person vocationally genuine. My soul's voluntary alignment to its inner whispered name is the most essential act of abandonment into the energy of God. The ear of my heart seeks attentively to hear the unique name by which the spirit of my being is called forth from a shadowy existence of accepted confinement into the vibrancy of life in abundance.

I can find it easy to accumulate projects and plans but fail to attend to the most pressing life project: to embrace our personal unique journey on the sea of God, a journey externalised by ancient Irish monks like Brendan of

Clonfert (*c*. 484 – *c*. 577). Setting aside my best-made maps is the first step in sailing to the guidance of the Spirit. On the silent open sea of the Spirit I become more finely attuned to the multiple subtle modes of guidance about when to swim or dive or sail or float. I awaken to the burning bush of presence in what previously had been perceived as simply the haphazard, random drama of unfolding life currents.

Dr Bernadette Flanagan is Director of Research at All Hallows College, Dublin City University and Co-Editor of Spiritual Capital: Spirituality in Practice in Christian Perspective *(2012, Ashgate). She has been pioneering the study of Christian spirituality in university settings for the past twenty years and is the convener of New Monasticism in Ireland.*

Her book Embracing Solitude: Women and New Monasticism *was published in 2013 by Resource Publications. New Monasticism is a movement turning to classical spiritual sources for guidance about living spiritual commitment with integrity and authenticity.*

TONY FLANNERY

Life After Death

MY MOTHER WAS within a few days of death, at the age of
ninety. She had been lapsing in and out of a type of coma
during those days. Occasionally she had lucid moments.
During one of those moments it happened that I was the
one sitting beside the bed. She gestured that she wished to
sit up. I helped her. She looked closely at me, and said:

'Tony, what is ahead of me?'

I had resolved that during this important time in her
life I would try to be as truthful with her as possible. I
answered:

'I don't know, Mum.'

'But you are a priest; you are supposed to know!' And
she fixed her eyes on me, demanding an answer.

'I don't know what is before you; but I believe it will

be greater and more wonderful than anything you could imagine.'

And I looked at her, hoping she would lapse into sleep and let me off the hook. But I could see she was thinking deeply. Eventually she let out a big sigh, and said: 'It is all a big muddle; some day I must sit down and work it out.'

She died two days later, not, of course, having worked it out. She went gently, and as far as I could make out, without any fear and with a sense of expectation of what was to come, and a readiness to be a part of it.

In the face of death maybe that is the best we can do. I have found it to be true that as I grow older the mystery of life and death deepens rather than becomes clearer. I have gradually discarded a lot of the notions and images of heaven, hell and judgment that I brought with me from my upbringing and education. My understanding of God, in so far as I can get my mind to grapple with the notion, has changed many times in the course of my life, and is now very different to what it was in my early years. That is only as it should be. Mystery should never be corralled into simplistic answers. But I have not lost the belief that there is something after death. In the course of my three score and six years on this earth I have discovered that life contains many beautiful and wonderful experiences. There are also, of course, many things that are hard and difficult. But part of the mystery is discovering that what appears to be tragedy can often turn out to contain within it a great blessing, a new growth, a new direction, maybe a new understanding. I am convinced that the most important achievement in life is precisely to grow in understanding.

All of this has taught me that the human mystery does not end in the grave; that our hearts are calling out for something more perfect and more permanent. That is why I told my mother that what she was entering into would be greater and more wonderful. I hope that it was so, and that I too, in my turn, will face it with the same equanimity that she did.

Tony Flannery is a Redemptorist priest and religious writer. A native of Athenry, County Galway, he founded the Irish Association of Catholic Priests and for many years has been writing a monthly article for Reality *magazine, published by the Redemptorists. Tony was suspended by the Vatican in 2012 for suggesting that, in the future, women might become priests, and calling for this and other matters to be open for discussion. He was told he could return to ministry if he agreed to write, sign and publish a statement agreeing that he would adhere to Church orthodoxy on issues such as women priests, contraception and homosexuality. He refused and remains barred from ministry. His response to this admonition came in August 2013 with his book* A Question of Conscience *(2013, Londubh Books).*

Maureen Gaffney

Think Carefully About What You May Regret In Life

WE MAKE A lot of decisions on the basis of trying to avoid regret. We especially fear that we will regret things if we later find out there were better alternatives. We are more afraid of accepting bad advice than rejecting good advice, more afraid of making a slightly risky bad choice than opting for a conventional choice.

Ask people to list the things they most regret in the past year or so and they mention 'acts of commission' – doing things that they wished they hadn't. You can probably think of your own list: eating too much at Christmas; that last unwise glass of wine; getting into a foolish argument with a colleague at work; buying the ten-year-old sports car that costs as much to run as a fleet of taxis and spends more time being repaired than on the road; losing your temper with your children; agreeing to join a committee that is now consuming far more time than you expected; and the all-time favourite, taking on way too many commitments.

But, with a little time to reflect, and looking back on our lives in a more considered way, the things we most regret tend not to be 'acts of commission' but 'acts of omission' – the things we could have done but didn't.

We didn't take the good advice to stay in school, or go back to college to get that qualification we always wanted. We baulked at taking the chance to start our own business, or to change jobs. We didn't take the time to tell particular people how much we loved them, or how much they helped us in our lives.

We regret not spending more time with our families and friends, and not relishing to the full the time we did spend with them.

Like many parents, I suspect, when my children were young, I never thought that these glorious years of Transformers and Barbie dolls, of going to amusement parks and family holidays by the sea would pass as quickly as they did. But correspondingly, I have no regrets that we regularly stretched our finances to breaking point to pay for great holidays together as a family every summer.

Why do we regret failure more than foolish action? Because the one reliable consolation in having acted foolishly is that we probably learned something valuable. But what lesson is there in *not* doing something, besides the knowledge that we should have acted?

Fundamentally, we are mistaken about what we will regret, says Gilbert in *Stumbling on Happiness*; we do not realise that 'our psychological immune systems can rationalise an excess of courage more easily than an excess of cowardice, we hedge our bets when we should blunder forward'.

The final step to a flourishing life is to cultivate that 'excess of courage' and nourish it with unrelenting optimism.

I leave the last words to David Landes in *The Wealth and Poverty of Nations:*

> In this world the optimists have it, not because they are always right, but because they are positive. Even when wrong they are positive, and that is the way of achievement, correction, improvement and success. Educated eyes-open optimism pays; pessimism can only offer the empty consolation of being right.
>
> The one lesson that emerges is the need to keep trying. No miracles. No perfection. No millennium. No apocalypse. We must cultivate a sceptical faith, avoid dogma, listen and watch well, try to clarify and define ends, the better to choose means.

EXCERPT FROM *Flourishing* (2011, Penguin Ireland)

Maureen Gaffney is an expert on change management, emotional intelligence, 'gender at work' and on work/life balance. A clinical psychologist, she has worked with companies in Ireland and further afield in the areas of leadership, change, emotional intelligence and managing diversity. She is a well-known Irish broadcaster, writer and columnist.

CARLO GÉBLER

WHY AM I HERE? For a start, because I was born when I was born. Middle of the twentieth century. A good time to come along. Plus, I was white and middle class. Modern medicine and good clean drinking water also helped. I was – I am – incredibly lucky. I didn't die, that's why I'm here, and it's all down to a sequence of benign accidents.

When I was younger I never thought much about chance. Now I do, constantly. That's down to another accident. In 1992 I was asked to replace a creative writing teacher in Her Majesty's Prison Maze (Long Kesh if you prefer) who'd suddenly left: the contract was for six weeks: long story short, those six weeks led to continuous employment, first in the Maze and latterly, twenty-one years later, HMP Maghaberry (where I still work, one day a week).

Prison has taught me many things: the most important is how close to catastrophe we all are. Oh, we think we're in control and safe and we've got it all sorted but many of the prisoners I meet (say half, maybe even two-thirds) have just had terribly bad luck. Oh yes, where others less fortunate are concerned we do well to remember the old cliché, 'There but for the grace of God go I.'

I could (we all could) so easily fall: it's important to remember that because it keeps you on your mettle. Also, if you really cleave to it, it impedes you (or at least it impedes me) from becoming a blowhard, from becoming one of those who big themselves up by passing judgment on those less fortunate than they are. That's why I keep telling myself, 'Dame Chance has largely smiled on you, pal, but she could so easily have frowned and don't you forget it.' It keeps me tender.

However, as well as believing it's all chance, I also believe in fixed duties which allow no room for chance. I'm particularly thinking here about my imagination, that fantastic faculty that when I read turns the words from a book into images that I can see on my inner cinema screen, and that when I write gives me my material as film scenes with the characters in costume, the rooms furnished and so forth on my inner cinema screen, and which I then turn into words that are then read and uploaded by the reader and turned back into images which they, the readers (because we all have imaginations) then see on *their* inner cinema screens. I've spent my life feeding, caring, developing and augmenting this faculty (which was the gift of my parents, both writers) because there is no alternative: it is my duty.

So, why am I here? Answer: to fulfil a non-negotiable obligation, the care of an imagination: or, if you prefer,

I'm here to write (which is what I do with my imagination) and when I write I make order and in a world where everything is chance, making order is the best comfort going.

Carlo Gébler is the son of writers Edna O'Brien and Ernest Gébler and was born in Dublin in 1954. He moved to London with his mother in 1958. He has written several novels and also a memoir about the relationship with his father – Father and I: a Memoir *(2000, Abacus) – as well as travel books and a book of history,* The Siege of Derry *(2005, Abacus), which gives an account of Derry's ten-day struggle against the Jacobite army in 1689. He lives in Enniskillen with his wife and five children.*

Maurice Guéret

Grave Matters

I AM THE family expert on matters pertaining to graves. The job description includes visiting old plots and finding those that are lost. Less frequently, it involves the planning of new ones. Graveyards have long been a source of comfort to me.

I do most of my visiting out of season and out of hours. On or near anniversaries, that sort of thing. I'll pull a weed or replace a vase. There are graveside mementoes to be surveyed, the shape and cut of the stones, and potted histories to be studied.

Then I'll take a moment to watch the sky, the lie of the earth or the sea if the resting spot is maritime. You are never stuck for neighbours in a cemetery. The dead are plentiful, and even living visitors might stop for a chat or pass with a nod. The headstones may carry a name you recognise, or a death more untimely and perhaps sadder than the others. The dates can be important – a time of epidemic perhaps, or a well-recorded disaster.

I have been known to visit graveyards on holidays, too. On a short romantic trip to Paris, I persuaded my young wife to spend a sunny spring afternoon wandering the long avenues of Cimetière du Père-Lachaise. She has not looked at me in quite the same light since. We found *beaucoup de Guérets*, and paid final respects to Oscar Wilde, Frédéric Chopin and Jim Morrison. The doctor in me made sure that we consulted a few deceased quacks too. Madame Guéret knows well that my comfort with the dead contrasts with an uneasiness when visiting living sick people in hospitals. Strange for a doctor perhaps, but hospitals fill me with a kind of miasma, a feeling of fear, foreboding and dread, a taste of bad air. My visits tend to be fleeting. Momentary episodes of grape-dropping or newspaper delivery. I'm quite happy to visit the sick in their homes or have them see me in the parlour. As a wise friend once said, 'sure aren't we all full of contradictions'. My short hospital career must have had its ghosts.

Might I be missed when my time comes? I walk a cocker spaniel seven days a week and have done so for decades. Were I to shuffle off early, there might be nobody to do the walking. Each week I pen a homespun column on *materia medica* for a Sunday newspaper. The cheque is not half as welcome as the letters from ordinary readers full of personal theories, ailments and remedies. It is my privilege to channel their wisdom, and perhaps this column might be missed by a few. And I read a chapter or two in a humorous voice to a beautiful daughter each night before she dreams. I might never be missed, except for that golden time.

Life after death would be wonderful. But I have learned that it doesn't pay to speculate. There will be ordinary footprints on my headstone. Dad, dog walker and doctor. Rest in Peace. But not just yet.

Dr Maurice Guéret is a well-known figure in Irish medicine. His mother dressed him in a dickey-bow from the age of four. A specialist in General Practice and member of the Society of Medical Writers, Maurice's humorous writings and original commentary on a wide range of materia medica *have inflamed colleagues and soothed patients for decades. See drmauricegueret.com*

'We make a living by what we get,
but we make a life by what we give.'

WINSTON CHURCHILL (1874–1965)

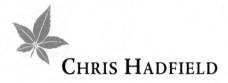

CHRIS HADFIELD

The trip takes a lifetime

ONE MORNING A strange thought occurs to me shortly after waking: the socks I am about to put on are the ones I'll wear to leave Earth. The prospect feels real yet surreal, the way a particularly vivid dream does. The feeling intensifies at breakfast, when reporters jostle each other to get a good photo, as though I'm a condemned man and this is my last meal. Similarly, a little later on, when the technicians help me into my custom-made spacesuit for pressure checks, the joviality feels forced. It's the moment of truth. The suit needs to function perfectly – it is what will keep me alive and able to breathe if the spacecraft depressurises in the vacuum of space – because this isn't a run-through.

I am actually leaving the planet today.

Or not, I remind myself. There are still hours to go, hours when anything can go wrong and the launch could be scrubbed. That thought, combined with the fact that I am now wearing a diaper just in case we get stuck on the launch pad for a very long time, steers my interior monologue away from the portentous and towards the practical. There's a lot to remember. Focus.

Once everyone in the crew is suited up, we all get into the elevator in crew quarters to ride down to the ground and out to our rocket ship. It is one of those space-age moments I dreamed about as a little kid, except for the slow – really slow – elevator. Descent from the third floor takes only slightly less time than it does to boil an egg. When we finally head outside to walk toward the big Astro van that will take us to the launch pad, it's that moment everyone knows: flashbulbs pop in the pre-dawn darkness, the crowd cheers, we wave and smile. In the van, we can see the rocket in the distance, lit up and shining, an obelisk. In reality, of course, it is a 4.5 megaton bomb loaded with explosive fuel, which is why everyone else is driving away from it.

At the launch pad, we ride the elevator up – this one moves at a good clip – and one by one we crawl into the vehicle on our hands and knees. Then the closeout crew helps strap me tightly into my tiny seat, and one of them hands me a note from Helene, telling me she loves me. I'm not exactly comfortable – the spacesuit is bulky and hot, the cabin is cramped, a distinctly un-cushion-like parachute and survival kit is wedged awkwardly behind my back – and I'm going to be stuck in this position for a few hours, minimum. But I can't imagine any place else I'd rather be.

After the ground crew checks the cockpit one last time, says goodbye and closes the hatch, it's time for pressure checks of the cabin. Banter ebbs: everyone is hyper-focused. This is all about increasing our chances of staying alive. Yet there is still a whiff of make-believe to the exercise because any number of things could still happen – a fault in the wiring, a problem with a fuel tank – to downgrade this to yet another elaborate dress rehearsal.

But as every second passes, the odds improve that we are going to space today. As we work through huge checklists – reviewing and clearing all caution and warning alarms, making sure the multiple frequencies used to communicate with Launch Control and Mission Control are all functional – the vehicle rumbles to life: systems power up, the engine bells chime for launch. When the auxiliary power units fire up, the rocket's vibration becomes more insistent. In my earpiece, I hear the final checks from the key console positions, and my crewmates' breathing, then a heartfelt farewell from the Launch Director. I go through my checklist a quick hundred times or so to make sure I remember all the critical things that are about to happen, what my role will be and what I'll do if things start going wrong.

And now there are just thirty seconds left and the rocket stirs like a living thing with a will of its own and I permit myself to move past hoping to knowing: we are going to lift off. Even if we have to abort the mission after a few minutes in the air, leaving this launch pad is a sure thing.

Six seconds to go. The engines start to light, and we sway forward as this huge new force bends the vehicle, which lurches sideways then twangs back to vertical. And at that moment there is an enormous, violent vibration and rattle. It feels as though we are being shaken in a huge dog's jaws, then seized by its giant, unseen master and hurled straight up into the sky, away from Earth. It feels like magic, like winning, like a dream.

It also feels as though a huge truck going at top speed just smashed into the side of us. Perfectly normal, apparently, and we had been warned to expect it. So I just keep 'hawking it', flipping through my tables and check-lists and staring at the buttons and lights over my head, scanning the computer for signs of trouble, trying not to blink. The launch tower is long gone and we're roaring upward, pinned down increasingly emphatically in our seats as the vehicle burns fuel, gets lighter and, forty-five seconds later, pushes past the speed of sound. Thirty seconds after that, we're flying higher and faster than the Concorde ever did: Mach 2 and still revving up. It's like being in a dragster, just flooring it. Two minutes after lift-off we are hurtling along at six times the speed of sound when the solid rocket boosters explode off the vehicle and we surge forward again. I'm still completely focused on my checklist, but out of the corner of my eye, I register that the colour of the sky has gone from light blue to dark blue to black.

And then suddenly, calm: we reach Mach 25, orbital speed, the engines wind down, and I notice little motes of dust floating lazily upwards. Experimentally, I let go of my checklist for a few seconds and watch it hover, then drift off serenely, instead of thumping to the ground. I feel like a little kid, like a sorcerer, like the luckiest person alive. I am in space, weightless, and getting here only took eight minutes and forty-two seconds.

Give or take a few thousand days of training.

EXCERPT FROM *An Astronaut's Guide to Life on Earth* (2013, Macmillan)

❧

Chris Hadfield is one of the most seasoned and accomplished astronauts in the world. He most recently served as Commander of the International Space Station, where he gained worldwide acclaim for his breathtaking photographs and educational videos about life in space. His music video, a zero-gravity version of David Bowie's 'Space Oddity', received over 10 million views in its first three days online.

In February 2013 he sent the first tweet in Irish from space with the words 'Tá Éire fíorálainn' and a night-time photo of Dublin.

On 13 May 2013, Hadfield landed in Kazakhstan after travelling almost 99.8 million kilometres while completing 2,336 orbits of Earth.

FIDELMA HEALY-EAMES

The Meaning of Life

> *True happiness comes from the joy of*
> *deeds well done, the zest of creating*
> *things new.* SAINT-EXUPÉRY

MY LIFE HAS always been a quest for meaning. That quest has been for different things at different times. It hasn't stopped. Every day I have a plan and the odd Saturday when I let myself off the hook my daughter Ruth still ensures I have one! A strong work ethic has always driven me, something bred into me growing up with my parents, my sisters and brother on a busy dairy farm in Moylough in County Galway. As I've gotten older I have learnt to stop, to enjoy silence and to reflect a lot more, enjoy nature, sharing time, to be more spiritual in essence. On the whole, though, I prefer to share life experiences than experience them by myself. Only this week I bought my husband a bicycle so that we could enjoy cycling together rather than my doing it alone.

Along the way I have been fortunate to have been able to touch many people's lives and many people have touched mine.

My story has similarities and differences to many people's lives. A lot of joy, pain too. Times when I pushed myself to the limit. In my twenties it was graduation from college, my first teaching job in Athenry, falling in love, an early marriage to Michael, emigration to the US, teaching in New York State schools and doing my Masters there. It was a real adventure. I felt invincible. Contrast that with the next phase when we came up against a wall of not being able to have children. I look back now and feel that my thirties were almost exclusively dedicated to having Niall and Ruth, both adopted, both teens and testing the hell out of us! But that is not entirely true. I continued to teach, move to teacher in-service education, various second-ments and completed a PhD in Education (National University of Ireland Galway) in 1999.

I was ambitious in education for the pursuit of excellence in my practice and in the learner. This gave my life a lot of meaning. I developed my own theories, formulated a view. At the end of 1999 I secured a post as a Lecturer in Education at Mary Immaculate College, Limerick. It was a dream come true. I loved my job educating young people to become teachers. It was a privilege.

In 2000 we adopted our daughter Ruth from Romania.

I felt complete. Although there are only 5½ years between Niall and Ruth the adoption process probably took ten years from start to finish. It was a long hard process, but a deeply meaningful one. Together we have often reflected on the magic of adoption, the selflessness of the natural mothers that gave their children to us, that as a family not one of the four of us is a blood relative. Amazing.

All was not to stand still. The three-hour round trip from Oranmore to Limerick every day with two young children and a demanding job took its toll. I had joined Fine Gael a number of years earlier and in 2002 I was asked to run in the general election for the Galway West constituency. In hindsight, it was sheer madness. Fine Gael had a desperate election and I was an unknown. Although I wasn't successful, I got the bug. I resigned my post in Limerick and set up my own business in education and training so that I could pursue politics. My forties were dedicated to politics, to public service and to Fine Gael. This year I will be ten years elected to politics – first to Galway County Council (2004–07) and laterally to Seanad Éireann. It hasn't all been plain sailing. As well as success there have been failures too, some very tough, especially the general election of 2011 when I was knocked out by fifty-six votes. Still, I learnt from it and moved on. I got a phenomenal vote in the subsequent Seanad election (2011), which helped a lot.

On reflection, I became active in politics because I felt I had been lucky in life. I was fortunate to have come from a strong, loving family. I had a good sense of self and I had benefited from a good education and earned a lot of positive reinforcement from my work and relationships en route. My husband Michael believed in me and supported my decision to go into politics. Fundamentally, I knew I wanted to make a contribution to my country and was driven by a motivation to serve and make a difference. This instinct persists. Only recently a friend asked me 'do you ever get sick of it?' (referring to politics). I heard myself answering 'yes, but my conviction is still bigger than any problem.'

It would be an understatement to say politics is easy. It is insecure and uncertain. So much is out of one's control and so many can be plotting against you at any given time. It is not easy on family and you can miss out on key moments. This is when you really question yourself. That said, there is also satisfaction to be had. I always get a sense of fulfilment out of being able to help someone, making headway on a project, organising a good event, pursuing a meaningful debate, contributing to a policy or working on my first private member's bill as I am doing at present.

It is exciting and deeply meaningful to think you can change practice for the better of your country, for its citizens, if your bill is passed into law. This will be my first bill as an Independent Senator since I was expelled from Fine Gael in July 2013, in the aftermath of the abortion legislation. This was a personally testing time but in the main I have no regrets. Hand on heart, I can say I weighed up the issue carefully. I made my decision to vote pro-life, to vote against the government and my own party on evidence grounds (there was none to support the Bill), on conscience grounds and on the basis that my party, Fine

Gael, had broken its pre-election promise and so was unaccountable to its electorate. In the end it was a matter of principle for me.

Since then life has changed considerably. I am a founding member of the new political grouping Reform Alliance. The seven of us are now working to create a new policy offering for the Irish people for the next general election. It is challenging. But part of my purpose in life is to be counted, to stand for something, to lead, not to follow. I am grateful to all those who support me and believe in me.

Fidelma Healy-Eames lives in Oranmore with her husband Michael, a farmer, and their two teenage children. She is a former lecturer, teacher in education and primary teacher as well as previously owning a small business in Education & Training.

She served on Galway County Council for the Oranmore area from 2004 to 2007 and also as the Fine Gael Seanad spokesperson on Education and Health (2007) and Social Protection (2013). In July 2013, Fidelma was expelled from the Fine Gael parliamentary party when she defied the party whip by voting against the Protection of Life During Pregnancy Bill 2013. On 13 September 2013, she and six other expellees formed the Reform Alliance, described as a 'loose alliance', rather than a political party.

MARK PATRICK HEDERMAN

THROWN INTO THIS world without my permission, I have come to recognise that the only thing that matters is doing what you were created to do in the first place. That may be a lifetime's work, or it may be one single task you are called to perform. All you can do is put yourself in the most appropriate position for reading the instructions, however quietly and unobtrusively these are delivered. I have placed myself in a monastery at Glenstal Abbey in very beautiful surroundings where I have lived for the last fifty years. It is a most privileged watchtower from which to read the signs of the times. This place, this structure, this way of life, makes it possible for me to hear the still, small voice of the reticent Godhead, punctiliously scrupulous about not forcing my free will. How is that voice heard most readily? In my experience, mostly through coincidence. Coincidence is God's way of prompting while remaining anonymous. I can be too impetuous by nature and have sometimes broken the starting gun. Experience teaches discernment, and finding yourself tediously on the wrong path, either as a victim of misunderstanding or misconception, hones your judgment and sharpens your antennae. So, at this point in my life, I never make any move unless it has been signed in triplicate by the three-personed God. But when something does happen three times I take it as a gentle hint that I am to do something about it.

Mark Patrick Hederman has been a monk in Glenstal for over forty years. Formerly headmaster of the school there, he has lectured in philosophy and literature in America and Nigeria, as well as in Ireland. He is the author of several books, including Kissing the Dark: Connecting with the Unconscious *(1999, Veritas),* The Haunted Inkwell: Art and our Future *(2001, Columba) and* Walkabout: Life as Holy Spirit *(2005, Columba).*

Ann Henning Jocelyn

AREN'T WE LUCKY to live in a society that recognises human and civil rights? That has laws to protect each citizen, from the most vulnerable to the most empowered, from crime and injustice, cruelty and abuse? Where we have universal access to health care and education, and a welfare system to ensure that we all receive what we are deemed to be entitled to?

Having said that, one human entitlement is rarely mentioned: the right for us all to flourish. Flourish on our own terms – that is, bring to fruition the essence of our finest qualities. Not as a form of self-indulgence, but to enable us to pass on whatever gifts we have. Just as the in-flight security announcement exhorts passengers travelling with small children to attend to their own oxygen mask first, we need to attend to our own inner welfare before we can be of any use to others.

My belief is that every individual born to this world, given the chance, has the potential to contribute something worthwhile. Yet we educate our children along narrowly defined parameters. Those who do not excel academically are systematically weeded out, starting in Junior Infants. We seem to overlook the fact that our world needs more than people with a retentive memory, with linguistic, mathematical or technical skills. The alternatives of artistic pursuits or practical skills come as a clear second.

Our culture seems to have forgotten all about fostering the best of human instinct, celebrating instead things like sex appeal, wealth, power and success. Rarely do we see a premium attached to assets such as the ability to listen and empathise, to help heal the wounds that are an inevitable part of life. But if we can aim to be a force for the good, our life will never be void of meaning. Conversely, if we lose sight of ourselves as having something of value to offer, we risk becoming depressed, even suicidal.

Even when we find ourselves in the most straitened circumstances, there is nothing to stop us from being generous with comfort, reassurance and encouragement. Just imagine how the world would be transformed if we could all avoid the pitfalls of envy, competition, bitterness and resentment and instead focus on bringing out the best in each person we encounter. Imagine the difference it would make to our own life if everyone we come across was bent on doing the same.

Whenever such support comes our way, it is invaluable: a bonus to be cherished. For our own part, if we make a habit of granting goodwill, it will spread like rings on water. One thing is certain: there will never be room for regrets. And when the time comes for us to depart from this life, we can take comfort from the fact that, whatever our personal limitations, the efforts we made will have left the world just a tiny bit better off than we found it.

Ann Henning Jocelyn had an early debut as a playwright in her native Sweden while completing a degree in Drama, which was followed by drama school in London. She has spent much time in Connemara, Ireland, writing books and plays that have been published and produced in many parts of the world.

Her contributions to the RTÉ programme A Living Word, *published as* Keylines for Living *(2007, O Books) have appeared in many languages, including Chinese.*

Ann Henning Jocelyn's most recent play Doonreagan *is set in Doonreagan House where she resides with her husband Robert. It is where the English poet Ted Hughes fled after the suicide of his wife, the poet Sylvia Plath. He was accompanied by his mistress, Assia Wevill, and her children. Doonreagan House now serves as a private residence as well as a retreat for writers and artists.*

TONY HUMPHREYS

JAMES HOLLIS, A Jungian psychoanalyst, writes about finding meaning in the second half of life. It certainly is the case that the first half of life is given over to finding security where one lives, works, plays and prays. In my own life, I asked the deeper questions in the first half of life, questions which have pursued me into the second half of life.

My entrance into a monastery when I was eighteen was a watershed experience. I have long known that it was an unconsciously desired creative strategy for me to 'leave the nest', as any other form of exit would have been difficult for me. During my seven years in the monastery I did have some spiritual experiences – transcendent moments of inner peace, a sense of oneness with all things and that everything makes sense. I might add that these special times did not derive from my then belief in

Catholicism, but from a pursuit of meaning to life. I gradually lost all my beliefs in Catholicism and left the monastery and the Church some few months before ordination. At that time leaving a monastery was socially taboo and I also became an 'embarrassment' to my family. Sadly, I was not in a place to empathise with their loss as I was faced at the age of twenty-five with the enormity of having no money, a black suit, no relevant education and no career. I also experienced quite deep depression and at times felt suicidal. After I left the monastery and after spending a couple of troubled weeks at home, I went to live in Dublin. I recall a lucid dream, which I can still clearly remember over forty years later. Indeed, dreams have had quite an influence in my life – especially at critical times – and became one of the foundation stones to an emerging spirituality. In the dream there was a great earthquake and people, including myself, were escaping up a mountain and I witnessed the people rushing to safety into a church on the mountainside. In the dream, I knew the church was going to collapse and I ran into the church and exhorted people to follow me up a path which would bring us to safety. As we climbed the path we looked down and saw it collapse into a pile of rubble. It was only later on in my life when I practised psychoanalytic psychotherapy that I realised the dream was symbolically communicating about the huge upheaval that had occurred in my life and my need to find my own life path and not rely on sources outside myself. The crowd of people represented all the parts of myself that were repressed and needed to emerge. I subsequently spent thirteen years in universities and pursued careers in education and in clinical psychology. During the course of the latter, I identified and resolved the unconscious sources of many of my fears. I continued to have some transcendent experiences, and questions on what life was all about were never far from my mind. But I became very busy with my career, marriage, writing books and newspaper columns, university lecturing, course designing and national and international engagements.

Three years ago I became quite sick, was initially misdiagnosed, wound up losing a lot of weight and was eventually hospitalised. In hospital, the initial diagnosis was that I had a terminal liver cancer, but after a week this was revised to my having an abscess in the liver arising from a chronic gallbladder infection. In spite of all the medical panic and the very deep concern of my partner and friends, I felt deeply at peace. I had three lucid dreams whilst in hospital. The first dream was where I was rushing to get to the airport and had somehow lost sight of a female colleague who was carrying my briefcase. I came to the top of a concrete stairway which had no guardrail. There were lots of people coming and going on the stairway and I began to rush down the steps whilst looking behind me to see if I could spot my colleague. A four-year-old boy running up the steps bounced off me and went plummeting over the side. I saw his head hit the concrete ground and I knew he was dead. This dream was attempting to bring to my consciousness how busy I had become, how I had stopped taking care of my inner child and kept losing sight of my feminine (heart) side. The dream was an alarm call.

On the same night I had a second dream: I was walking down an old cobbled street in Cork and came to a twenty-foot sheer wall that could not be scaled. I needed to go forward – there was no going back – and I stretched my arms upwards and found myself floating up and over the wall. I had no doubt that this dream was letting me know that, though I was encountering a serious health challenge, I would rise above it and emerge well.

A third dream – same night – was where I was in my late eighties and attending a social function. People were telling me how well I was looking and one person said 'and you know what would help is a bit of lipstick'. The message here was that if I stuck to my word and found my heart and cared for myself, I would live healthily into old age.

Dreams always amaze me. Here we are, fast asleep, and the Self that I believe each one of us is never sleeps and creates the most astonishing scripts, scenarios and actors to bring something to our consciousness. Crises in life are another means that the Self employs to bring essential matters to our consciousness. Life for me is about coming to consciousness of one's individuality, power beyond measure, truth, sacredness, our infinite nature and eternal presence.

Dr Tony Humphreys is a consultant clinical psychologist, author, and national and international speaker. He works with individuals, families, schools, local communities and

the business community. He is Director of three National University of Ireland courses which are run in University College Cork and in an outreach centre in Dublin. He is co-founder of the Irish Association of Relationship Mentors.

'Nothingness is the sister of possibility . . .
When you feel nothingness and
emptiness gnawing at your life, there
is no need to despair. This is a call from
your soul, awakening your life to new
possibilities. It is also a sign that
your soul longs to transfigure the
nothingness of your death into the
fullness of a life eternal, which no
death can ever touch.'

JOHN O'DONOHUE (1956–2008)

Jonathan Irwin

'How do you do it?'

A frequent question to the worn-out parents of children with severe disabilities, whose primary aim is to keep their child warm and cosy at home where they belong. Precious children who typically can't walk, talk, who may be blind and deaf, who are oxygen dependent, fed through a tube and who are totally dependent on their parents and carers to get them through the day. Literally.

Friends stop calling because they don't know how to help. It's awkward. Overwhelmed by the harrowing routine of caring for this damaged child at home. Normal family life stops. Siblings grow up overnight. Quickly sensing the priority given to their sick brother or sister.

Getting out the door for work is like a marathon. Grocery shopping is a luxury. As for a weekend break, well, that would be equivalent to winning the lottery!

Yet, the vast majority of families want their sick child at home. The child does much better medically, emotionally and socially outside the sterile hospital ward. Being at home is a tonic.

Underneath all of this disability, there is a baby who wants all the cuddles and comfort of home life. A child with no ego. No expectations in life. No grudges. No worries. When he's in pain, he cries. When he's not, he's happy. Pure happiness. For whatever short time he has. And he takes a part of your heart that you didn't know existed.

I know because I'm Jack Irwin's dad. Born on 29 February 1996 and left brain-damaged after a seizure in the hospital nursery, Jack beat all the odds. This wise little man convinced his mum and dad to take him home, against the advice of our doctor who said our family would not cope, as there were simply no services for Jack outside the hospital.

We didn't know what we were doing but cope we did, just about. With the help of family and friends in our neighbourhood. Rallied by a local nurse who had the kindest compulsion to step in and to rescue us. An angel who cobbled together a homecare plan for our Jack.

It wasn't ideal and it was tough. But there were flashes of pure magic. And we always knew it was the right thing to do. Jack found his sanctuary in the bath, his favourite place on earth. And I heard my son chuckle. Only once. But it echoes in my heart forever.

At the age of twenty-two months, Jack died at home, leaving his dad with clear instructions to bring more children home. That's Jack's legacy. And that's my job.

Since 1997 we have supported 1,700 families to bring their children home. They baffle the doctors, doing much better and deriving some inner strength from being at home, amongst their family and friends. Others are brought home to die but truly leave their mark and take their place in the family home, snapshots of happiness on the mantelpiece. Pioneers, like Jack.

So how do their parents cope? They do it because they have to. They do it because they can. With a little bit of support from the Jack & Jill Foundation – funded by the generosity of the Irish public – they cope.

And so do I.

Jonathan Irwin is Founder and CEO of the Jack and Jill Foundation. Educated at Eton and Trinity College Dublin, he has occupied many roles – bloodstock agent, auctioneer, stud owner, publisher and racetrack and sports executive (the British Bloodstock Agency, the Phoenix Park Racecourse, Dublin Sports Council and Special Olympics).

In 1997 Jonathan and his wife MaryAnn O'Brien – MD of Lily O'Brien's – set up the Jack and Jill Foundation, based on their personal experience with their son Jack who died that year. The foundation has helped over 1,700 children since 1997. The service includes financing of practical home nursing care, home visits by one of its liaison nurses, practical advice on care for the child, listening to the family and making representations on their behalf.

Jonathan was named Rehab Person of the Year in 2004.

Jennifer Johnston

WHY AM I HERE? I have to say, I haven't the foggiest idea. It seems to me a pointless question; well, anyway, a question to which I have not heard or read any sensible answer. A question which I in my old age stopped asking; life has become too short to run in circles looking for answers to unanswerable questions. It is best to get on with what you do best, try and do it better, whether it is being a high court judge, or a cake maker, an actor, doctor or road sweeper or, like myself, a writer, a juggler of words; there are always more things to learn, most of them to do with communicating with other people, talking, listening, hearing, watching, laughing, crying if need be, and understanding. Perhaps I should say 'trying to understand' because sometimes it is very difficult to go the whole way. This is where my work begins, trying to put what I have learned about people into the characters about whom I write, their truths and untruths, their sorrows and joys. The great writers seem to be able to do this with such ease, the rest of us come panting along behind, doing our best, for that, after all, is all you can do. I think that every human being has the gift of creativity inside; for some, the lucky ones, it is just below the surface and dances into the bearer's life with energy; for the rest you have to dig, but it is there waiting to be released. Once you have discovered this gift you life will change, it doesn't necessarily mean that you will suddenly begin to write books or paint pictures, compose music or anything like that, but you will look at the world in a different way; you will receive grace and joy and understanding from just being alive, but I bet you still won't know why you're here.

Dubbed the 'quiet woman of Irish literature', Jennifer Johnston is often under-appreciated for her low key and personal stories, although peers such as Roddy Doyle acknowledge her to be one of Ireland's finest writers. A late starter, she published her first book at the age of forty-two, but from the outset her distinctive talent was apparent. Many of her novels deal with the fading of the Protestant Anglo-Irish ascendancy in the twentieth century.

Johnston has won a number of awards, including the Whitbread Book Award for The Old Jest *in 1979 and a*

Lifetime Achievement Award from the Irish Book Awards in 2012. The Old Jest, *a novel about the Irish War of Independence, was later made into a film called* The Dawning, *starring Anthony Hopkins.*

FERGAL KEANE

Letter to Daniel

Hong Kong, February 1996
Daniel Patrick Keane was born on 4 February 1996.

MY DEAR SON, it is six o'clock in the morning on the island of Hong Kong. You are asleep cradled in my left arm and I am learning the art of one-hand typing. Your mother, more tired yet more happy than I've ever known her, is sound asleep in the room next door and there is soft quiet in our apartment.

Since you've arrived, days have melted into night and back again and we are learning a new grammar, a long sentence whose punctuation marks are feeding and winding and nappy changing and these occasional moments of quiet.

When you're older we'll tell you that you were born in

127

Britain's last Asian colony in the lunar year of the pig and that when we brought you home, the staff of our apartment block gathered to wish you well. 'It's a boy, so lucky, so lucky. We Chinese love boys,' they told us. One man said you were the first baby to be born in the block in the year of the pig. This, he told us, was good Feng Shui, in other words a positive sign for the building and everyone who lived here.

Naturally your mother and I were only too happy to believe that. We had wanted you and waited for you, imagined you and dreamed about you and now that you are here no dream can do justice to you. Outside the window, below us on the harbour, the ferries are ploughing back and forth to Kowloon. Millions are already up and moving about and the sun is slanting through the tower blocks and out on to the flat silver waters of the South China Sea. I can see the contrail of a jet over Lamma Island and, somewhere out there, the last stars flickering towards the other side of the world.

We have called you Daniel Patrick but I've been told by my Chinese friends that you should have a Chinese name as well and this glorious dawn sky makes me think we'll call you Son of the Easter Star. So that later, when you and I are far from Asia, perhaps standing on a beach some evening, I can point at the sky and tell you of the Orient and the times and the people we knew there in the last years of the twentieth century.

Your coming has turned me upside down and inside out. So much that seemed essential to me has, in the past few days, taken on a different colour. Like many foreign correspondents I know, I have lived a life that, on occasion, has veered close to the edge: war zones, natural disasters, darkness in all its shapes and forms.

In a world full of insecurity and ambition and ego, it's easy to be drawn in, to take chances with our lives, to believe that what we do and what people say about us, is reason enough to gamble with death. Now, looking at your sleeping face, inches away from me, listening to your occasional sigh and gurgle, I wonder how I could have ever thought glory and prizes and praise were sweeter than life.

And it's also true that I am pained, perhaps haunted is a better word, by the memory, suddenly so vivid now, of each suffering child I have come across on my journeys. To tell you the truth, it's nearly too much to bear at this moment to even think of children being hurt and abused and killed. And yet, looking at you, the images come flooding back. Ten-year-old Andi Mikail dying from napalm burns on a hillside in Eritrea, how his voice cried out, growing ever more faint when the wind blew dust on his wounds. The two brothers, Domingo and Juste, in Menongue, southern Angola. Juste, two years old and blind, dying from malnutrition, being carried on seven-year-old Domingo's back. And Domingo's words to me, 'He was nice before, but now he has the hunger.'

Last October, in Afghanistan, when you were growing inside your mother, I met Sharja, aged twelve. Motherless, fatherless, guiding me though the grey ruins of her home, everything was gone, she told me. And I knew that, for all her tender years, she had learned more about loss that I would likely understand in a lifetime.

There is one last memory. Of Rwanda, and the church-yard of the parish of Nyarabuye where, in a ransacked classroom, I found a mother and her three young children huddled together where they'd been beaten to death, The children had died holding onto their mother, that instinct we all learn from birth and in one way or another cling to until we die.

Daniel, these memories explain some of the fierce protectiveness I feel for you, the tenderness and the occasional moments of blind terror when I imagine any-thing happening to you. But there is something more, a story from long ago that I will tell you, face to face, when you are older. It's a very personal story but it's part of the picture. It has to do with lines of blood and family, about our lives and how we can get lost in them and, if we're lucky, find our way out again into the sunlight.

It begins thirty-five years ago in a big city on a January morning with snow on the ground and a woman walking to hospital to have her first baby. She is in her early twenties and the city is still strange to her, bigger and noisier than the easy streets and gentle hills of her distant home. She's walking because there is no money and everything of value has been pawned to pay for the alcohol to which her husband has become addicted.

On the way, a taxi driver notices her sitting, exhausted and cold, in the doorway of a shop and he takes her to hospital for free. Later that day, she gives birth to a baby boy and, just as you are to me, he is the best thing she has ever seen. Her husband comes that night and weeps with joy when he sees his son. He is truly happy. Hung-over, broke, but in his own way happy, for they were both young and in love with each other and their son.

But, Daniel, time had some surprises in store for them. The cancer of alcoholism ate away at the man and he lost his family. This was not something he meant to do or wanted to do, it just was. When you are older, my son, you will learn about how complicated life becomes, how we can lose our way and how people get hurt inside and out. By the time his son had grown up, the man lived away from his family, on his own in a one-roomed flat, living and dying for the bottle.

He died on the fifth of January, one day before the anniversary of his son's birth, all those years before in that snowbound city. But his son was too far away to hear his last words, his final breath, and all the things they might have wished to say to one another were left unspoken.

Yet now Daniel, I must tell you that when you let out your first powerful cry in the delivery room of the Adventist Hospital and I became a father, I thought of your grandfather and, foolish though it may seem, hoped that in some way he could hear, across the infinity between the living and the dead, your proud statement of arrival. For if he could hear, he would recognise the distinct voice of family, the sound of hope and new beginnings that you and all your innocence and freshness have brought to the world.

EXCERPT FROM *Letter to Daniel – Despatches from the Heart (1996, Penguin Books).*

Fergal Keane is a Dubliner, one of four children. His father, Eamonn, was an actor, successful but dogged by alcoholism, which wrecked his marriage and caused a twenty-year separation from his son. The other key male figure in his life was his uncle, the renowned playwright, John B. Keane.

Before joining the BBC in 1989, Keane worked for the Cork Examiner, The Irish Times *and RTÉ. At the BBC, he worked in Northern Ireland, South Africa and Asia, moving to Hong Kong and then returned to London to be based in the BBC's World Affairs Unit.*

He has published widely, including The Bondage of Fear: A Journey Through the Last White Empire *(1995, Penguin),* Season of Blood: A Rwandan Journey *(1996, Penguin),* Letters to Daniel: Despatches from the Heart *(1996, Penguin) and* A Stranger's Eye *(2001, BBC Audio Books).*

Keane was awarded the Amnesty International Press Award in 1993 and an OBE in 1996. He lives in London.

COLM KEENA

SOME SAY THE great question is why is there something rather than nothing? To my mind it is a question to which we don't have an answer. Any move onwards from this to a belief in God just begs the question. Furthermore, given all the sorrow, hardship and suffering there is in the world, believers are faced with why any god would create such a cruel world. I think we live in a godless universe.

It does not follow that our lives are meaningless, although, surely, many lives have been, are, and will be.

I think it is important to put the question of meaning in a context. Back in our hunter/gatherer days, when our emotions were evolving, we collected food for later, collective, consumption. Our inner, emotional lives reflect this history. It is why we have emotions such as suspicion, generosity, selfishness, and a sense of fair play. We need to look out for ourselves while acknowledging that we can only flourish through cooperation. This is the basis of political philosophy (and why we are angered by non-tax resident billionaires). It is the context within which we live and within which we can find meaning.

One of the key characteristics of life is the influence of positive and negative loop systems, both in terms of our dealings with others, and our interior lives. In terms of the latter, this is why how the world appears to us can be hugely influenced by our interior motivations. A man or woman who strives to be decent sees the decency of others more easily than a person more driven by selfishness or envy. Life can appear more meaningful to a person who tries to be good.

I am wary of linking legacy with the idea of life's meaning. Think of 'patriots' who espouse violence against their fellow countrymen; or Christians who put loyalty to the Church before the suffering of the individual. Our minds are wonderfully slippery.

I think people can be saved, so to speak, by striving to be well-mannered, kind, respectful of the feelings of others. I think these related capacities grow with effort, much in the way, say, that practice makes a better hurler or piano player. Striving in this way can contribute to the ability to feel, and receive, love. Negative, selfish motivations can close a heart down.

The whole idea of this book – what gives life meaning – stems for our inbuilt propensity to look for meaning, which, in turn, I suspect, is a function of our capacity for grammar. We like our sentences to make sense. Grammar is one of the great evolutionary wonders of the world.

People have a profound need to communicate. We should chat with each other. It is a comfort.

And then there is gladness. What does it matter if we don't know why there is something rather than nothing, if we are glad? Gladness trumps meaninglessness, and its great beauty is that it does not require a reason.

There is something else to say about gladness, kindness, goodwill, and love. They are commonplace.

Colm Keena is Public Affairs Correspondent with The Irish Times *where his areas of interest include business controversies and the interaction between business and politics. Keena's report in 2006 about the Mahon Tribunal's inquiries into payments to the then Taoiseach Bertie Ahern created a political crisis. His refusal to cooperate with the tribunal's inquiries into the source of the information in that report eventually led to a Supreme Court ruling governing the right of journalists to protect confidential sources of information.*

Keena has written books on Charles Haughey, Bertie Ahern and Gerry Adams as well as on the secretive banking system that operated during the Haughey era known as the Ansbacher Deposits.

DAVID KELLY

IN 2013, CANADIAN astronaut Chris Hadfield had many of us enthralled with his stunning photographs of Planet Earth, taken from the International Space Station. The extraordinary beauty and colour of the planet had the effect of compelling us to stand back from our many concerns in life, if only for a brief moment, and look at our world from a different perspective. In such moments we can sense, perhaps for the first time, the real beauty of the world in contrast with the myriad problems that beset us on its surface. If only we could resolve our problems, wouldn't our world be as beautiful on its surface as it is from outer space? It sets one thinking: what is life all about? Why are we here? Indeed, why am I here?

As a Catholic priest and a member of a religious community, my ministry is essentially that of a carrier of the good news of the gospel of Jesus Christ. Yet I am conscious that many people carry burdens that weigh them down with unhappiness: family and relationship issues, economic burdens, health problems, addictions and suicide, especially among the young. Clearly, it would be hard to blame people in such situations, if they were to seriously question the purpose of life and wonder why they are here at all. Such problems suggest there is much darkness in life. Yet, even in darkness, there are chinks of light occasionally, hints of something better, the possibility of hope and the hopefulness of possibility. I recall from the 2012 Paralympic Games in London the extraordinary achievements of many athletes despite their physical disabilities; their victories of courage; their belief in what might be possible. I take great hope and encouragement from such achievements.

People, such as myself, have the blessing of a religious faith to bolster hopefulness and a belief that life, despite all its travails, has meaning after all, even if we only have so many years in this world of ours. My faith points me to the ultimate hope of life beyond this life, with a God of love and a community of saintly women and men, those who have gone before me on the journey. This is what helps me to make sense of life here in this world, insofar as it is possible to do so. Life beyond life in a real sense starts here, with myself, as I try to keep faith with a journey that springs from faith. I do not undertake this journey alone. My fellow pilgrims, even those who might not share my religious outlook or acknowledge the existence of God, are my companions on the journey and it is they who help to give me reason and purpose for being here on the planet. They help me to bring whatever light and hope there are to those without light and hope. That is why I am here.

David Kelly is a priest and a member of the Augustinian Order (OSA) and is based at St John's Priory, Thomas Street, in Dublin. He is a lecturer in theology and spirituality at the Milltown Institute; a visiting lecturer at All Hallows College and St Patrick's College, Drumcondra, and at the Loyola Institute (Trinity College Dublin). For many years he has also been involved in giving retreats to religious communities and to lay groups in Ireland, Northern Ireland and in England.

'I *am the captain of my fate*
I *am the master of my soul.*'

WILLIAM ERNEST HENLEY (1849–1903)

HARRY KENNEDY

WHY AM I HERE? There are questions like this that only occur to you when you find yourself by accident standing in a Romanesque cathedral in Burgundy, or a perpendicular Gothic cathedral in the Fens. I recently found myself in such a space in Barcelona – Santa Maria del Mar – built in 1329 and improved by a fire in 1936 that stripped out the Baroque vanities added later.

The question 'why am I here' is too large – it has to be broken down.

Where am I? I am now probably past the middle of my life expectancy, but still some way from retirement. I can no longer complain about the way things are run and done, because for some years now, my friends, my contemporaries and even I myself have been in charge of most of the things I want to complain about.

Where was I? I recently reviewed a history of the 163-

year-old hospital where I work. I read the pithy dismissals of my predecessors – Dr X 'reforming', Dr Y 'regressive'. The distillation of decades of each person's work into several words was daunting. A century of perspective left none of my long-gone colleagues looking 'progressive' unless they were given the lame apology 'for their time'.

So why am I here, working in a forensic psychiatry hospital under the eye of a judgmental future and a capricious, critical present?

Every year the hospital admits people who have fallen through every safety net of the mental health services, the criminal justice system and the cohesion of their own communities. They arrive tormented by passions, psychic pain and confusion. The more disturbed they are on arrival, the more dramatic the improvement by the time they are ready to depart. Most are returned to their families after a month or two. Some have to stay in the hospital for many years. Unsafe anywhere else, they live large parts of their lives with a dignity that is dependent on the safety we provide for them and for those who care for them. Yet the patients we work with are the most interesting and the most complex in medicine and the most needy. They need to be recognised as people with disabilities they themselves have not caused or chosen, people capable of recovery, and people with their own stories to tell.

The work my colleagues and I do is only possible when one abandons moral judgment and concentrates instead on some objective recognition of the person living out a mental disability that might be alleviated to some extent by a humane, supportive and safe environment, through nursing care that is kind, skilled and wise, some medical science and quite a lot of professional commitment.

These vanishing hospital skills are in need of conservation now, like the construction of drystone walls and blacksmithing. Now and then, my colleagues and I find ways of improving this art. Modernising and reforming is a process rather like the 1936 fire in Santa Maria del Mar.

Professor Harry Kennedy is a forensic psychiatrist and the Clinical Director of the Central Mental Hospital in Dundrum. He distracts himself by seeing patients, concentrating on epidemiological and medico-legal research and playing loud music.

MARY KENNEDY

Mam's Copybook

> *Life, we've been long together.*
> *Through pleasant and through cloudy weather:*
> *'Tis hard to part when friends are dear*
> *Perhaps 'twill cost a sigh, a tear.*
> *So steal away, give little warning.*
> *Choose your own time.*
>
> ANNA BARBAULD (1743–1845)

IT'S A VERY strange feeling to be reading through someone else's personal things. Someone who is no longer with us, was much loved and whose death has left a gap in the lives of her family and friends. It forces you to ask yourself some hard questions: should I be opening these pages and reading anything I find? Would it be better just to throw it all away? Or should I consign it to the back of the bookshelf or the attic maybe? No, I don't think so.

The hardback copybook, with yellowed, lined pages contains cuttings and thoughts my mother began to collect when she was a young woman. I discovered them in the chest of drawers in her bedroom after she died when we had the horrible task of clearing her house before selling it. Some are clippings from newspapers, sellotaped in position, others are written in her lovely handwriting, with a fountain pen, like the extract at the beginning of this piece from a poem called 'Life' by Anna Barbauld.

My mother chose to write the whole of that poem into her copybook before she was married. She was young and healthy. And as I read it now after she has lived her life and died I look on it in a very personal way. It's a poignant reminder of those heartbreaking and lonely days when she died. I realise that if she chose to collect this piece it was because it was meaningful for her. This is what she believed. There's no fear of death here but an acceptance, which is not surprising given my mother's deep faith and belief in life after death.

For me, it's a pleasant reminder of the reality of life: sometimes pleasant, sometimes cloudy. It's a reminder of the gift of friendship. But most of all it's a reminder that death is inevitable, outside our control. It will happen. So we should make the most of our time on earth, enjoy the good things, cherish the friends and live life to the full.

These sentiments are clearly visible in another poem Mam included in her copybook. It's called 'Had I But One Day' and is a salutary reminder that we take so much for granted in life and that we should make the most of every minute we have on this earth.

Had I but one day of life remaining,
Then should I see this generous world I love,
The dawn, the noon, the glorious colour staining
The western sky, the stars serene above
With clearer eye than ever I employ . . .

I should be much more eager to forgive
And sympathise, and help and love and pray,
Before the numbered hours had hurried past.
And that is what they must mean when they say
Live every day as if it were the last.
ANON

The contents of my mother's hardback copybook are full of sound wisdom and full of beauty. They are uplifting and offer insight into the kind of person she was in so far as these were the thoughts she liked to think. It is nice to read them again and to quote some of them here. In a way it's like breathing new life into these thoughts, the ones that strike a chord with me.

Life is mostly froth and bubble,
Two things stand like stone.
Kindness in another's trouble
Courage in one's own.
ANON

Kindness was one of her defining features. She would never listen to gossip or innuendo and thought the best of everyone. There's a piece she chose to include in her book that I really like and which illustrates that personality trait. It's called 'Narrow Hearts' by Jean Morton and it laments the fact that some hearts are so narrow that they have no time for fun or for friends.

> *What a pity some hearts are so narrow*
> *That they've little room for a friend*
> *So little room for the grace of life*
> *And so little hope to lend.*
> *So little understanding,*
> *So little help to spare.*
> *So little room for Life's tender things*
> *In which every heart should share.*

The first two stanzas are taken up with the tender things that a person with a closed or narrow heart is missing out on. And then comes the hope.

> *But even the narrowest heart we'll find*
> *Will warm at somebody's touch.*
> *So when in Life's walks we encounter*
> *A heart that is cramped and sour*
> *Let us leave just a smile and a prayer*
> *And hope in the end they will flower.*

She quite simply loved people – all people. She was kind, loyal and loved company and a good laugh. In fact, there's a piece she included that is very telling. It's something Lord Macmillan said and Mam obviously found it very meaningful.

One should take good care not to grow too wise
For so great a pleasure of Life is laughter.

EXCERPT FROM *Lines I Love* (2007, Merlin Publishing)

Mary Kennedy is a presenter with RTÉ. She has worked on a variety of programmes, including Open House, *the* Eurovision Song Contest *and* Up for the Match. *She currently presents* Nationwide *on RTÉ One. She is the author of three books:* Paper Tigers *(2003, Merlin),* Lines I Love *(2007, Merlin) and* Lines for Living *(2012, Hachette).*

SR STANISLAUS KENNEDY

A Vision of Social Justice for the Future

WE CAN ALL recognise the value of a socially just society, where people's needs are met and no one is excluded on the basis of cultural and economic difference, but until we acknowledge our greed and let go of it, we will never attain social justice. We also need to let go of our fear of people who are different from ourselves, of our contempt for people from a different background, and our tendency to blame people for their poverty. We need also to let go of our overweening ambitions for ourselves and our own children at the expense of everything else.

Divesting ourselves of these negative values – greed, selfishness, fear, contempt, feelings of superiority – and replacing them with values of justice, equity, inclusion and collectivism may seem impossible. We look at how society works and we think: it can't change, we are too closely wedded to our own interests, it's human nature to be competitive and to exclude others, it's just the way things are. But it is not necessarily so. If we are prepared to envision a different way of living, and to articulate that vision and reiterate it over and over again, we can win hearts and minds. It is possible to persuade people to change their views and their ways of living. In the past, people thought that many things would never change and they did. Women got the vote, for example, though it must have seemed impossible to most people in the nineteenth century; other enormous changes in gender politics followed so that now women own property independently of their fathers and husbands, work in whatever jobs they are suited to, and play their part in the life of society outside the home. On a smaller scale, who ever would have believed ten years ago that Irish people would virtually unanimously and with little argument accept the idea of a ban on smoking in pubs?

As new ideas are discussed and publicly debated, people think about them and see their merits, and gradually, over time, social attitudes change. Some social changes come about as a result of a sudden event or series of events; some come about partly because of legislation or because as a society we sign up to international treaties and agreements such as the Declaration of Human Rights; but in the end social change comes because people want change, they see the value of change and they make a collective decision to accept and implement it. I believe that my vision of a socially just future for Ireland is not an impossible dream.

It is up to us all, politicians and people, to think about it, talk about it and come up with the mechanisms for bringing about what amounts to a social revolution. We need to overhaul the infrastructures of our society and put in place infrastructures that will support social justice.

EXCERPT FROM *The Road Home: My Journey* (2011, Transworld)

Sr Stanislaus Kennedy is a social innovator and political activist who has dedicated her life to the fight for a more equitable society and service to the poor. Inspired by Mary Aikenhead, who founded the Religious Sisters of Charity, she is the founder of Focus Ireland, now the biggest national organisation for the homeless; Young Social Innovators, which provides social awareness education for 15 to 18-year-olds; and the Immigrant Council of Ireland, a human rights organisation that promotes and supports the rights of immigrants.

Her latest project is the Sanctuary Meditation Centre, a place of meditation and contemplation in the middle of Dublin city centre. Sr Stan wanted the Sanctuary to provide people with an opportunity to find sanctuary in their own lives, no matter who they are.

Mary Kenny

I WAS A LATE child, and it is sometimes a source of wonder (and gratitude) to me that I am here at all. My father was 67 and my mother 42 when I was born: I had three older siblings, all born more than a decade before me. My mother frankly confessed to me that she was dismayed when she discovered she was expecting another baby after ten years without a pregnancy. In fact, she believed she was entering the menopause when menstruation ceased, and indeed, after I was born, in 1944, she immediately experienced the menopause.

So I arrived on this earth via the Last Chance Saloon, biologically speaking – with that little flare of fertility that arises before close of play . . .

And bless them, my parents probably were a little too old to start raising a child: my father then died when I was five: and the family fortunes deteriorated financially.

I was wild, from the start, but often regarded as a special child too – perhaps because of my unexpected appearance in the family. I bellowed at my christening, making sure I was noticed. I nearly died from choking as an infant: it just happened that there was a medical student visiting the house, who held me upside and managed by some stratagem to dislodge the obstruction in my throat just as I was losing the ability to breathe. At four, I had a serious pneumonia. I almost lost an eye in a reckless childhood game. I ran over a high parapet unharmed. I swam across a dangerous whirlpool at the age of 11, and survived.

My Guardian Angel was frequently on high alert duty and brought me through. Now I am nearly at my seventh decade I often count my blessings and look back with gratitude. Life can be very unfair: bad things happen to good people – other members of my family who deserved to live long and fulfilled lives very sadly departed before their time. Those of us who have been spared to live the Biblical three-score-year-and-ten need to be thankful for the privilege, and do our best to live each day as best we can in an act of gratitude.

I left school early and had to make my own way in the world from the age of 16, so I have a chip on my shoulder about not being well-educated: but an inferiority complex carries the compensatory element of propelling us to try harder. I yearn to make the best of myself, to self-improve, to seek for higher goals and greater ambition, and achieve the fullest potential that I can on this earth. Though I rebelled in youth, and still resist conforming to all norms

– I wear purple rather than beige – I appreciate greatly the deep kindness that was my family's enduring characteristic. The Catholic faith they practised was not a narrow and oppressive one, but generous, warm, charitable, and merry. It was also cultured. I am here to serve that legacy as best I can.

Mary Kenny has been a journalist since the 1960s and now qualifies as a 'veteran', thankfully still in harness. She has written for over thirty newspapers and magazines in Ireland and Britain.

She was one of the founding members of the Irish Women's Liberation Movement and, in 1971, travelled with Nell McCafferty, June Levine and other feminists on the 'contraceptive train' to buy condoms in Belfast, at that time illegal in the Republic of Ireland. In the 1990s she developed an interest in social and biographical history, and published an acclaimed study of Irish values in the twentieth century, Goodbye to Catholic Ireland. *She subsequently published a biography of William Joyce,* Germany Calling, *which was made into a television documentary for the History Channel, and her play about Winston Churchill and Michael Collins,* Allegiance, *was performed to full houses in Edinburgh in 2006 with Mel Smith and Michael Fassbender. Her book* Crown and Shamrock: Love and Hate between Ireland and the British

Monarchy *(2009, New Island Books) details Ireland's relationship with the British monarchy.*

She is married to the writer Richard West and both their sons are writers and journalists. She lives 'between England and Ireland', in Kent and Dublin.

Colum McCann

SHE FELT SUDDENLY grateful. You wake one morning in the howl of a northern Missouri winter, and moments later you are on the deck of a transatlantic cruiser, and then you are alone in Rome, and a week after that you are in Barcelona, or on a train through the French countryside or back in a hotel in St John's watching a plane break the sky, or in a hat shop in St Louis watching the rain come down outside, and then, just as suddenly, you sit in a hotel in Ireland watching your daughter across the lawn, moving between the ice sculptures, passing a tray of champagne amongst a hundred wedding guests. Emily could sense the skip in her life, almost like the jumping of a pen. The flick of ink across a page. The great surprise of the next stroke. The boundlessness of it all. There was something in it akin to a journey across the sky, she thought, the sudden shock of new weather, a wall of sunshine, or a pelt of hail, or the emergence from a bank of cloud.

She had a sudden urge to write to Teddy Brown and tell him that she understood entirely now, in this raw moment, why he did not want to fly any more.

EXCERPT FROM *TransAtlantic* (2013, Bloomsbury)

Colum McCann was born in Ireland in 1965. He is the author of six novels and two collections of stories. He has been the recipient of many international honours, including the National Book Award, the International Dublin IMPAC Prize, a Chevalier des Arts et Lettres from the French government, several European awards, the 2010 Best Foreign Novel Award in China, and an Oscar nomination. His work has been published in over thirty-five languages. He lives in New York with his wife, Allison, and their three children.

Place your mind before the mirror of
  eternity!
Place your soul in the brilliance of
  glory
Place your heart in the figure of
the divine substance
and through contemplation
transform your entire being
into the image of the Godhead Itself.

St Clare (1194–1253)

ELEANOR MCEVOY

WHY DO I EXIST? In truth, I don't know why: it's for greater minds than mine to determine the 'why' of existence, but to me, to some degree, it is irrelevant. The fact is, I do exist. The challenge is to find meaning for myself in that existence.

In the words of Gabriel García Márquez, in his novel *One Hundred Years of Solitude,* 'It's enough for me to be sure that you and I exist at this moment.'

Doing the best that I can do and being the best that I can be helps me find meaning in existence. Giving and receiving love, an embrace at the end of a long day, a walk through a forest with my daughter, a bottle of wine in the company of close friends, an audience at one with a musical phrase, the excitement of writing a song that touches the soul in a way that I can't quite comprehend . . . all of these things serve to provide meaning to my life.

After I've gone, I guess my legacy will be that I will live on in the hearts of those who remember me. Perhaps I will live on in the hearts of those that remember my music. Whatever lives I have touched, for good or for bad, they will remember me and for good or for bad, that will be my legacy.

Over the years, I have come to see the importance of 'living' a life, rather than 'postponing' a life. All the time, I hear people say 'I'll do that when the kids are older', 'I'll do that when I lose weight', or 'I'll do that when I have the money'. Time and time again, I have to apprehend myself when I hear myself say 'I'll do that as soon as I get off the road, once I get home'. The fact is that if you want to make changes to your life, or to do something you're passionate about, you have to seize the moment and do it now. I now write letters and post them when I'm travelling. I no longer wait till I get home, because in my experience, by the time you've arrived home, other mundane tasks surface and you're bogged down by the everyday, nitty-gritty to-do list.

As I grow older, I am more aware of how enormously precious time is. I'm more conscious of the importance of good health and I'm increasingly grateful for the extra-ordinary life I have had. My appreciation for my loved ones has grown over the years and my definition of success has altered so dramatically that it bears no resemblance to my youthful perception of the same.

Every night as I go to sleep I think of three things that I'm grateful for that day, and I think of something that I am looking forward to the next day. It only takes a moment, but for that moment I focus on what is important in my life and what gives a value to my life. I am very fortunate that I have so much to be grateful for.

Eleanor McEvoy was born in Dublin and loved music from the very beginning. When she was four, she started piano lessons. At age six, she took up the violin, and joined the Junior Irish Youth Orchestra at thirteen. After school she went to music college and played in pit orchestras in her free time. After college she was accepted to the National Symphony Orchestra, with which she played for four years until she decided on a career in pop music.

MEDBH MCGUCKIAN

IT IS HARD to be alive in 2013 if you have been alive for more than half a century and Seamus Heaney has died. He was the one that gave meaning to many thousands of us. We have to learn to access that meaning in a non-physical way. I am not sure I am living my supposed life. But when I am writing I am sure I am. To be useful, Oscar Wilde says, is to be beautiful. What is useful is that I can create that beauty in my work, even if I cannot preserve it in me, except through my daughter. I can encourage young students to create it in their words. My legacy will be, I hope, to my children, some security. Hopefully my books and poems, some of them. I do believe in the reality of our 'life' beyond although I have little idea of its shape or what element we will breathe in or whether we will breathe. I think of the Risen Christ and how He ate bread, which seems natural enough. It influences my life here in that I never as yet totally despair, in that I pray to my dead and particularly to Our Lady of Perpetual Succour who is often very powerful when all else fails. My writing ability sustains me and binds me with that spiritual world in all sorts of ways and I aspire to help others by my language and by my forays with the unknown, as Heaney's voyage with the dark guided and helped us all. And continues to do so.

Medbh McGuckian was born in 1950 in Belfast where she continues to live. She has been Writer-in-Residence at Queen's University Belfast, the University of Ulster, Coleraine, and Trinity College Dublin, and was Visiting Fellow at the University of California, Berkeley.

The numerous awards she has won include: England's National Poetry Competition, The Cheltenham Award, The Rooney Prize, the Bass Ireland Award for Literature and, in 2002, The Forward Prize for the Best Poem for 'She is in the Past, She Has this Grace.'

Her most recent collection of poems is The High Caul Cap *(2012, Gallery Press). Medbh is a member of Aosdána.*

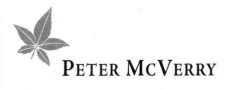

PETER MCVERRY

THE HUMAN RACE is one messed-up family. All around us we see homelessness, people who are stressed and depressed, children who are going to school hungry; on our television screens we see the victims of war and violence and natural disasters. A huge amount of suffering. And most of it is unnecessary.

For me, the purpose of life is to leave the world a better place than we found it. Other people, their suffering and their happiness, gives meaning to my life. We all have an innate sense of compassion: when we see a child suffering, something stirs within us, our hearts go out to that child and we wish we could do something to take that suffering away. This sense of compassion belongs to us as human beings, even before we become Christians or Muslims or Hindus or whatever. Religion can give meaning to our compassion but it is not the source of our compassion.

God is a large part of my life, a God who is compassion, a God whose passion, like every parent, is the children. I imagine God looking down at our world, seeing 1 billion people on our planet living on the edge of destitution, seeing people sleeping on our streets, seeing people fleeing from violence and war. And each of these people is God's beloved child, loved with an infinite love. God, too, suffers from the suffering of his children. God wants nothing more than that the human family of God would live together in peace and dignity. And that's where we come in.

Those who are suffering or homeless or in poverty offer us the greatest gift anyone can offer us – they invite us to open our hearts to include them in our love. If I expand my heart to include them in my love, then I become a more loving person, and therefore more human (and therefore more divine). My own happiness and fulfilment is ultimately, and intimately, linked to the happiness and fulfilment of others. As the African proverb says: 'If your neighbour is hungry, your chickens aren't safe!'

Love is expressed more in deeds than in words. And love is our greatest fulfilment. Any two teenagers, locked in an embrace they wish would never end, know that. They wouldn't swap that moment for all the PlayStations in Ireland – or even the latest iPhone. And the greatest suffering is to see the one we love suffering in pain. I am the luckiest person alive; I often say that I must be one of the few people in Ireland who actually *wants* to get up in the morning; the job satisfaction I get is second to none. But I get angry. I am angry at the unnecessary pain inflicted on those around me. I am conscious that most of the time I am incapable of taking that pain away. To do so requires major changes in the economic, social and political structures which contribute to that pain. Those structures are built on the attitudes (and sometimes on the apathy and prejudices) prevailing in society. To reach out to those in pain is necessarily to challenge and inform those attitudes. I cannot work with homeless people without seeking to change, not just their world, but the world around them also.

Is there life after death? For many people in our world, there is no life before death. The God I believe in calls me, not to turn in on myself and focus on what I have to do to get into Heaven, but to focus on others and what we can do to help each other.

The human race is one messed-up family. We have to try and heal the broken relationships that threaten the very survival of the human race.

While working as a priest in the inner city in Dublin, Fr Peter McVerry SJ encountered some homeless children and opened a hostel for them in 1979. He subsequently opened twelve more hostels, three drug treatment centres and ninety apartments. The organisation he started has now been renamed Peter McVerry Trust. He has written about his experience in a book The Meaning is in the Shadows *(2003, Veritas). His most recent publication is* Jesus: Social Revolutionary? *(2008, Veritas).*

ROISIN MEANEY

Right Place, Right Time

WHY AM I HERE? Good question. (I just typed 'God question' by mistake – talk about a Freudian slip of the finger.) Of course, it's also an unanswerable question – how can we claim to know with any certainty why we are here without knowing who, or what, got us here in the first place? And I'm assuming we won't discover the answer to *that* one until we aren't here any more. So instead of getting bogged down in philosophical mire, maybe I'll just look at where I am today and take it from there.

Where I am is a full-time writer, having taken the scenic route from my childhood dreams of being a vet or a dentist. As it turned out I became neither: instead I chose teaching, mainly because both my parents had taught, and

166

also because I enjoyed the company of children. Despite these somewhat flimsy reasons for my choice I spent several happy years in the classroom, but ultimately left it behind because I wasn't organised enough to be as fine a teacher as I wanted to be, and also because I had discovered something I loved more.

When I announced to my parents in 2008 that I was giving up my permanent, pensionable job to write books for a living they threw up their hands in horror, despite the fact that I had already managed to get three novels published in my spare time, but my gut was shouting at me to do it. I had no dependants apart from my cat, who didn't seem bothered whether I taught or wrote as long as she got fed, so I obeyed my gut, and so far neither of us has starved.

The twenty-first century is a wonderful and scary place. Wonderful because of how far we have travelled in terms of technology and science, scary because of how this knowledge is often used to destroy rather than create or enhance. War in all its futility terrifies me; violence in any form makes me recoil in horror. But I believe in the inherent goodness of people, and I choose to regard evil as an aberration that sometimes happens because we haven't been paying enough attention.

I also believe in an afterlife. I was brought up in the Catholic faith, and the idea that there is some kind of God, and some kind of heaven, pleases me. I look forward to asking God lots of questions, and I live in hope that I will get all the answers.

As a writer I have no job security, no guarantee at the end of a publishing deal that I will secure another, no film studios lining up (yet) to make me a million. Life as a writer can be isolating and frustrating, and it challenges me every single day. But since my first book was published in 2004 I have received countless messages from people who have read and enjoyed one or more of the books.

I am doing what makes me happy, and getting paid (a little) for it, and managing to make others a little happy too. I am truly blessed, and grateful.

Kerry-born Roisin Meaney finished a sentence and won a car when she was eighteen. Since then she has written ten adult novels and two children's books. She lives in Limerick city with a rather large cat, and enjoys the sweet things in life.

The beginning of Roisin's writing career is like a story from one of her novels. In winning Tivoli's 'Write a Bestseller' competition in 2002, she bagged a two-book deal and a dream start to her writing life.

Rónán Mullen

'LOVE AND DO whatever you please' is one of my favourite quotes. It comes from St Augustine and it might contain the solution to a lot of conflict.

As a practising politician trying and frequently failing to practise Christianity, I often hear that religion should be left out of politics. Religious inspiration is seen as a weak and controversial basis for identifying the common good. Since no two people have quite the same faith and many people have no faith, how can you 'impose' your faith-based views on anyone else?

The answer of course is that nobody should 'impose' their views on anyone. We live in a community. We need a certain minimum of rules for our protection. And we need at least majority support for those rules. But all we can do is 'propose' our best assessment of things. If you have religious reasons for believing something, and I have another kind of reason for believing something else, it doesn't follow that my reason is better than yours if I am not religious. After all, your religious views might cause you to seek fairness at all times. My non-religious views might be based on prejudice, self-interest or a harsh upbringing. Who is to say that I am being any more logical or fair-minded than you are?

Perhaps the important questions are (1) do we each sincerely believe in what we are saying, and (2) can our ideas be understood and shared by other people who are trying to be reasonable?

If we could get to that point, maybe we would have less bullying and name-calling in public debate. We would approach issues and problems with a genuine thirst for knowledge, wisdom and truth.

Personally, I wonder, though: if you don't have a deep-down religious basis for thinking what you really think, what is the source of your inspiration? What causes you to decide that murder is wrong, or that you should vote to help countries in the developing world, or invest in better education for our country's children, or hospice services for people with terminal illness, etc.?

Isn't a religious inspiration of some kind at the root of all good decision-making? It is fine to be polite and not belch publicly in restaurants because we wouldn't like other people to do that in our company. But what about those decisions where we ourselves don't win or lose in the short term?

If you believe in a loving God, it should follow that you would try to promote love of your neighbour in all you do, including in your laws. If you don't believe in a loving God, you might be tempted to believe that we are all just chemicals and that nothing really matters.

And yet many people who are unmoved by the formal practice of religion or notions of a relationship with God still want a better world. They try to live not just for themselves, but for others.

We are not doomed to conflict. There is Love. Though we don't hear much talk of it in politics, the idea of believing in Love may be a powerful place to start. Not a shallow, self-centred version of love, but the real stuff that invariably involves self-sacrifice. For the believing Christian, it should be a no-brainer. The full quote from St Augustine is this: 'Love God and do whatever you please: for the soul trained in love to God will do nothing to offend the One who is Beloved.' If we love God, there won't be any difficulty about morality. Love of God will lead us to act in loving ways. Not just towards God, but to others.

And that is where we can meet those who may not believe in a higher benevolence that wills and wishes the best for them. With St John, believers might say that 'God is Love'. With an equally sincere heart, non-believers might say that 'Love is God'. Countless people of all persuasions yearn for a better world, where there is fairness, justice and, above all, Love. That's the common ground where people of faith and the sincerely unreligious can meet in mutual respect. And try to know each other better.

꒰❀

Rónán Mullen hotly disputes Henry Kissinger's assertion that '90% of politicians give the other 10% a bad name', believing that the correct ratio is probably 80 to 20. He began his public life when he was elected President of the Students Union in NUI Galway for the academic year 1991/92. It was the beginning of a long, learning curve about the workings of media with which he has been more or less involved ever since.

Since getting his Masters in Journalism from Dublin City University, he has worked as an English and French teacher, a college administrator, a spokesman and press officer for the Archdiocese of Dublin, a barrister, a weekly columnist in the Irish Examiner *and* Irish Daily Mail, *a lecturer in Law and Communications, and member of the Seanad for the National University of Ireland since 2007.*

Senator Mullen denies that all this is proof of professional attention deficit disorder, claiming instead a fertile mind and wide range of interests. He admits that a lot of these jobs have involved talking for a living, something that comes of no surprise to those who taught him. 'He rarely stopped talking during class,' says his former teacher, John Walsh of Holy Rosary College, Mountbellew. 'And he was no bloody good at woodwork either.'

'To make the right choices in life, you have to get in touch with your soul. To do this, you need to experience solitude, which most people are afraid of, because in the silence you hear the truth and know the solutions.'

DEEPAK CHOPRA (1947–)

MARIE MURRAY

'IS IT YOURSELF'? What a powerful Irish interrogative. Equally profound and in the same genre is the observation 'I'm not myself', which is both a statement and explanation with which clients often begin psychotherapy as a way to define the angst of not knowing how to go on in an altered self.

Implicit in the question 'is it yourself' and the statement 'I'm not myself' lies the belief that there is an enduring identity or sense of self that is recognisable to oneself and to others so that when it alters radically it calls core personal identity into question. It conjures up ideas of having 'lost' oneself, of trying to reclaim or recoup the self, of there being a coherent 'self' with which one is content and another 'self' with which there is dissatisfaction. When we are rejected by others our 'self' is rejected, which calls for examination or restoration of that self. Self-esteem is but acceptance and celebration of one's 'self'.

And if I am 'not myself' then who am I? Is the condition of not being oneself a temporary condition to be tolerated until the return to one's 'real' self? Is it a plea to be reunited with one's ordinary, ongoing, recognisable, identifiable self? And when other people view us as 'not ourselves' from what does that derive? Is that a misconstrual, a stereotype that demands that we conform to a persona that we reject? Is it misunderstanding by others of who I personally believe that I am? One protests 'That's not me' when a description is foisted upon one that is dissonant with one's own construction of self. Are our 'true' selves those inner selves not visible to the outer world but 'authentic' existential and ontological selves encountered in deep moments of solitude and reflection? And what about the multiplicity of selves that we inhabit over a lifetime, conscribed by age, social circumstances and context, 'as many selves as there are individuals who know us' to paraphrase one of the grandfathers of psychology, William James, or, in the words of Shakespeare, the many parts we play as 'we strut and fret our hour' upon the stage.

What about the postmodern self, or 'selves', the social media selves that must coexist as we grow 'closer and closer apart', intimate strangers with innumerable others but essentially alone, dependent on how we are viewed and construed by those who have power to define us. The head hurts with questions when we excavate these caverns of thought about who and what we are, why we are here, what meaning our lives have in this world and what legacy we may leave behind.

Why am I here? Why am I here? Why am I here? What is the meaning of this life, this one and only life that I live now, at this time, in this place, in the world? The old metaphysical question 'why is there something rather than nothing' opens up questions, not just about the meaning of life itself, but about the meaning of our own individual lives. How do I make sense of my life, endow it with meaning, imbue it with purpose, honour it as gift, conduct it with dignity, relinquish it with belief that it does not end but alter when this time is done?

Each life, whether momentary or extended, is signifi-cant. We arrive into the world at a particular historical juncture so that life cannot be lived separately from the time in which it is lived, the people with whom it is shared, the family home, the school, the physical environment, the mental milieu, the social domain and the dominant discourses of the era. We think and talk, reason and ruminate and try to determine if our inner life is like the lives of other people. We try to make sense of tragedy and to recoup psychological equilibrium when we are shocked, bereaved, saddened, under threat, assaulted by nature or by each other, or by the sheer act of living life itself. Life is lived thought by thought, emotion by emotion, event by event: personal, public, each hour, each day, each week, each year, while what makes it meaningful changes shape and substance until we expire.

What matters to each of us may differ or differ at different times in our individual lives. What matters are memories, a word, a sentence, an emotion, a poem, an exchange, a silence, a book with tissue-thin pages, a child-hood toy, a Connemara wall, a word of praise, a feeling of regret, a crumpled note yellowed with age, a melody that repeats in the head, the snatch of a song, change of key, a look, a laugh, a pet buried, a parent mourned, a place, a gate, a detail, an event, a piece of clothing, a birthday card, a drawing on the fridge. And interwoven with all our esoteric memories are the lives of others with whom we have shared our lives.

Like others, I have woven the strands of my own personal and professional life into meaning, for how can any of us live our lives if life does not have purpose and intent? Motherhood has allowed participation in giving life. Being a clinical psychologist has provided a theoretical framework within which to interpret the inner world and it has also provided privileged access to the worlds of others during their times of greatest mental vulnerability and mental strength. The joy of journalism is that it has provided a way of translating these experiences into words, selecting them, examining them, altering and adjusting them, playing with them and presenting them and hoping that through them some articulation of some aspects of our human experience may emerge that may resonate for listeners and readers. The academic world has provided the opportunity to transmit what I have learned. Living brings understanding of life.

The legacy? Can any one of us answer that? Perhaps that as a writer a sentence may have encouraged, reassured or resonated. As a teacher that something said may have been new, or interesting or inspirational. As a psychologist that words may have allayed distress or regret, sadness and fear and enabled someone to 'find' themselves again. But therapy, like life, is not something that one does; therapy is about what one is. The therapist is created by the client, the teacher by the student and the writer by the reader. The psychotherapist, to quote psychologist Millar Mair, has to 'listen to the lilt and rhythm, to the use of words and phrases, the telling metaphor, the silence and the moving spaces in between'. Doing so unites all the questions to be addressed in this short piece; the question of identity, the question of life, the question of its meaning, its purpose, its work and its legacy.

And at the end of life I do not think that there is a full stop, maybe a comma, a pause before another existent stage. Maybe there is a semicolon; a punctuation to connect independent clauses with each other. Or perhaps at the end of life, we encounter a colon: that which marks a major division to indicate that what will follow is an elaboration, summation or implication of what has gone before.

Dr Marie Murray has worked as a clinical psychologist for almost forty years and is former Director of Psychology and Director of the Student Counselling Services in University College Dublin. She has contributed to many RTÉ Radio One programmes (including Today with Pat Kenny *and* Drivetime with Mary Wilson*). She has published two books based on her* Irish Times *column:* Living Our Times *(2007, Gill & Macmillan) and* When Times are Tough *(2011, Veritas).*

Nóirín Ní Riain

Why Am I Here?

WHEN I SEE or hear the word 'here', I immediately interpret it as a homophone which is a word pronounced the same as another, but with an entirely different meaning. So for this little reflection, I am taking 'here' to mean, not 'in this place or space' but, that which is aural, perceived by the ear, in other words, that which is listened to. Furthermore, I believe that sowing meaningful life seeds in the 'here/hear and now' is all about a certain kind of listening which is in the realm of the Divine.

There is something essentially spiritual about our sense of hearing. When we really listen – 'with the ear of the heart' as St Benedict calls it – to one another, to the cosmic sounds around us, to the sound of silence, we are inevitably tuning in to 'the deep heart's core' – another way of describing the presence of the One within. The ear, according to eighteenth-century Danish philosopher Søren Kierkegaard 'is the most spiritually determined of the senses'. Two centuries later, in 1985, Joachim Ernest Berendt agreed that hearing is 'the most spiritual of all the senses'. Moreover, he warned that favouring the visual and the visible in all areas of life has generally 'despiritualised our existence'.

'Listen so that you may live' is the late eighth-century BCE prophet Isaiah's invitation to abundant life (Isaiah 55:3). Well schooled and familiar with this marvellous, ancient, audio-centric, sacred Hebrew Book of Isaiah, Christ takes up the invitation. When great crowds from every town around gather to listen to him, the Divine Story-teller once again weaves a mystical verbal cloak around them all about a seed sower (Luke 8:1–15). But the underlying message for 'anyone who has ears to hear'(Luke 8:8) is around this radical sonic attention to the word of God. The storyteller goes on to unravel the seed-story for the stubborn, unimaginative disciples who have no idea what he is getting at.

The seed is the symbol for a new word – 'Theosony' (from Greek *Theos* meaning 'God' and *sonans* Latin for 'sounding'). What follows, as Jesus spells out in magnificent human psychological awareness, is firstly a three-fold definition of poor theosonic listening and then the true prescription for listening as the only way towards an open, honest and good heart.

When cosmic evil thrives and walks on our path, the sound of God is drowned out, not even a faint echo of it is to be heard. Secondly, when the seed lands on the rock, we listen for a while but ultimately give up and give way to the next fad or the next diet. Thirdly, the thorn-seed is choked by all sorts of distractions, consumerism and power struggles and although the whisper remains, it is garbled and gibberish.

However, the real theosonic genius is the one who, in the heart-silence, hears the Divine Word/Sound loud and clear and can 'hold it fast in an honest and good heart, and bear fruit with patient endurance/openness' (Luke 8:15).

We are here to grow where we are well and truly planted; to listen that we may live.

Nóirín Ní Riain is an internationally acclaimed spiritual singer who has recorded several CDs and is also author of books and articles. A theologian and musicologist, Nóirín was awarded the first ever Doctorate in Theology from Mary Immaculate College, University of Limerick, in 2013. Her thesis subject was 'Towards a Theology of Listening', for which she coined the term 'theosony'.

Nóirín has performed extensively worldwide. Notable events include the International Peace Gathering at Costa Rica to introduce His Holiness the XIV Dalai Lama in 1989, the United Nations Summit at Rio de Janeiro 1992 and the UN Earth Summit in Copenhagen in 1995. As a child she often visited Glenstal Abbey in Murroe,

Limerick, to listen to the chants of the Benedictine monks, later performing and recording with them.

She performs with her sons, Eoin and Mícheál Ó Súilleabháin, under the name A.M.E.N. and gives workshops about sound as a spiritual experience.

CHRISTINA NOBLE

MY WORK WITH the poorest of the poor takes me into some of the worst areas of Saigon, or Ho Chi Minh City as it is now officially called. It was in one of these that I first came across Phuc and his family, down by the railway tracks in Nhieu Loc, the city's canal district, a place more squalid than any shanty town, where people live in constructions like cages, one on top of the other. In the midst of the congestion I noticed something that looked like a small coal box – just a few boards of broken wood nailed together. I might have mistaken it for just that had it not been for a piece of old curtain hanging over the entrance. As soon as I saw that, I knew there was a woman inside.

I pulled back the curtain, peering into the blackness, and I was hit by the foul stench of human flesh. A family of five were hunched inside: a father and mother, two little girls and a young boy of about ten. The box was no more than 4 feet square, smaller than many Western toilets. So small, in fact, that there was no room to lie down – the family had to sleep sitting up against the walls.

My eyes went to the boy because, unlike the others, he was not sitting but lying on his back, motionless, with his matchstick legs drawn up towards his chest. A closer look told me he had cerebral palsy.

I was appalled by what I saw. Even the streets and alleys would have been a much healthier place to live. Tears sprang to my eyes and I wanted to be sick, but I knew I mustn't: it would only add to the humiliation these people were already feeling. So I swallowed hard and fought back my emotions.

I was with my Vietnamese colleague Helen Thuong. 'Helen,' I said, 'please ask the father if I can speak with him.'

The father came outside. He was about thirty-five, very neglected-looking and thin. The mother and children looked neglected and worn too, but the father looked worse. Instinctively I knew that if there was any food to share, he was the type of man who would let his wife and children have most of it. I was struck by the pain in his eyes and the lack of hope in his voice when he spoke to me – his low self-esteem.

My first reaction was to do something immediately, to take them out of this hovel, this box, but I knew it was impossible. 'Could you come to the Children's Centre at 38 Tu Xuong Street in District 3?' I asked him through Helen. 'I think we might be able to help you.'

He looked somewhat taken aback but with great dignity he nodded and said 'Yes.'

I asked him if I could see the whole family. Very politely they came outside. The two little girls, ragged but beautiful, stood looking at me, mystified by this yellow-haired stranger who was talking to their father. The father carried the little boy out, and I was immediately struck by the tender way he lifted and held him. I could see that he often did this by the way the boy's arms automatically went around his father's shoulders. The little boy's name was Phuc, we were told.

Then I saw the back of Phuc's head. It was not rounded, as it should have been but almost flat. Phuc had spent all of his short life lying on the ground. His body was twisted from head to foot and as frail as a five-year-old's.

Phuc's parents came to my office at the Foundation that afternoon. 'Please sit down,' I said. I could feel their embarrassment, and I understood it only too well. The Vietnamese are a gentle people, but they are very proud, and this family were obviously the victims of circumstance. I explained to them that I too had been very poor when I was a child. I too had lived in terrible conditions with my own brothers and sisters.

'Please don't be embarrassed,' I said, 'just tell me how can I help you? What do you need most?' I felt almost silly asking. I could see that this family needed everything.

The father said, 'I need a job.'

'What kind of job? What can you do?'

'If I had a Honda-om [a taxi],' he said, 'I could be a Honda-om driver,' but he shrugged as he answered, as if it was an impossible idea. He didn't even have food, never mind his own taxi.

'OK,' I said. 'Let's talk tomorrow. Could you and your family be at my office by half past ten? I'll send the Foundation van to pick you up, if that's all right with you.'

'Yes, yes,' he said, without any hesitation this time.

Next morning at 8.30 a.m., we had a meeting of the Foundation staff. Helen Thuong, our Vice-Director, chaired the meeting since she had already met the family and could explain the situation to the Vietnamese. Then we started the brainstorming.

Mr Nam, the senior social worker, was the first to speak. 'Before we do anything, we must check out their story, Mama Tina, to make sure it's true. How do we know they don't have a house they rent out while living in that box, or something else like that?' Nam knows his job and takes it very seriously. I always find him very reassuring. As an orphan and former street child he has the same eagle eye and experience as myself. He also has a great soul and a good brain.

'I know what you're saying, Nam,' I said, 'but, believe me, these people are genuine.'

We agreed that Phuc's father's idea of getting a Honda-om was a good one and I asked Quoc, our minibus driver, to find a second-hand one in good condition.

We all agreed that housing was a priority, and that for the sake of their health, we had to act fast. No decent person could leave them living in those conditions. But could we afford to rent them a big room, putting down at least one year's rent in advance?

I looked across at Mr Hai, our accountant, a man always in control, never fazed. 'Well, Ma'am,' said Mr Hai, 'you always say to us, if we don't have it, we must find it. And I can say to you, Ma'am, we can do. Yes, we can afford.'

'I love you, Mr Hai,' I said, 'because you always give me good answers.'

At half past ten, little Phuc and his family arrived. We told the parents about our meeting and asked them what they thought. It was difficult for them to take in what we were saying.

'We would like to arrange for Phuc to go to our Physiotherapy Unit in Phuang District for an assessment,' I said. 'If he goes, Dr Loc there will take good care of him.' In Vietnam, there is neither the knowledge nor the equipment to care for children with cerebral palsy, but I was hoping that Dr Loc might be able to suggest some kind of long-term rehabilitative programme. They also agreed that they and the little girls would have a medical check-up at our health clinic. But when I offered to look after Phuc full-time at the clinic until I could find them a room, they both shook their heads. It would be for only a matter of weeks, I explained, until we could find them other accommodation, and in the meantime we would give Phuc proper nourishing food. The answer was still 'no': Phuc was their son and they wanted to take care of him themselves.

When we gave the Honda to Phuc's father he just stared at it. I gave him the papers and suddenly his face broke into a huge smile.

'I hope it will earn money for you,' I said. 'Give you some independence.'

We found a piece of land just outside the city. It was cheap, about €2,000 with a little green field around it, which we would be able to buy for the family, thanks to a generous sponsor, who insists on remaining anonymous. We invited them all to come out in the van with us to see it and give us their opinion. It was their choice. Then we all piled into the van for the half-hour drive. There was a tremendous sense of excitement. I was holding Phuc in my arms and telling him and the two little girls where we were going. The children couldn't understand what I was saying but they knew from the way I was saying it that it was something good.

The van left the city behind and we turned off the main road into a country land. We stopped and parked. The children pressed their faces against the window, staring out. I wondered what they were thinking. I handed Phuc to his father, and the little girls and I held hands and skipped through the grass to the little plot of land. Their parents followed with Phuc, and while they were talking to Helen, I took him in my arms again. He was moving his head from side to side, squinting up at the vast blue sky, gazing up at the great arc of blue, utterly transfixed. He had never seen such space or light before.

I laid him gently down and guided his hands over the grass while his little sisters stood staring at him, obviously amazed. Phuc was pulling at the grass, holding it, his fingers exploring with incredible intensity. There was a gentle wind blowing and he seemed to be bathing in it, almost as if he could see it and touch it. His head, his eyes and his whole face were moving. It was as if, after ten years of lying in the dark like a corpse, Phuc had come to life.

I left the family and walked away across the fields. At moments like this I thank God for the dream that guided me to Vietnam. I feel that I'm the one who has been given the greatest gift.

The family liked the plot. With help from volunteers they built their home within a month and moved into it. Phuc's mother takes great pride in the little business she now runs, selling her home-grown flowers from a roadside stall. His father goes into the city each morning to work with his blue Honda-om, and when he has some spare time he helps us at the Foundation.

Physiotherapy and a good diet have done a lot to ease Phuc's condition. Last time I saw him at the Foundation he was in a snazzy new wheelchair and he was wearing a baseball cap just like any other cheeky ten-year-old. He and his sisters have the chance to be children now.

So I'd say my philosophy isn't just about mending bodies. It's about restoring people's independence, giving them a life, not just an existence. It's about respect and love and dignity. Those are the things we owe our children. Children are the ones who need them most of all.

ADAPTED EXCERPT FROM *Mama Tina* (1999, Corgi)

Christina Noble was born in the slums of Dublin. At the age of ten her mother died and her alcoholic father could no longer care for her or her siblings. In the years that followed she suffered physical, emotional and sexual abuse in orphanages and on the streets, and after her marriage she was the victim of domestic violence. One night in 1971 she had a dream about helping the street children of Vietnam and decided to make it a reality. In 1989 she set up the Christina Noble Children's Foundation in Ho Chi Minh City and in 1997 she expanded to Mongolia.

The movie of Christina's life, Noble, *was released in September 2014. Directed by Stephen Bradley and starring Deirdre O'Kane in the title role, it tells the story of a woman who believes that it only takes one person to make a difference.*

BREDA O'BRIEN

I AM HERE to serve. These were the first words that popped into my head after I received the request to write an answer to the question, 'Why am I here?'. The response startled me, because I know I am not a particularly selfless person. In my family, my husband is the one who serves others in every circumstance, whether it be an interaction in a shop, or the meals that appear every day on the table, or the fact that underwear drawers miraculously refill just as you have begun to notice that you are running out.

Our children slag him mercilessly about knowing the life story of every shop assistant who has ever served him, and for doing things like delivering home-made Christmas puddings as a thank-you to the local butcher and other shop owners. Our eldest son once teased his father for being the kind of person who would be inclined to ask others not to look too harshly on Judas Iscariot, because he probably had reasons for acting the way that he did.

Given that standard, and being much more often the recipient of service than the giver, might explain why I was surprised by my instinctive response. It reflects whom I would like to be more than who I am. But ideals matter. I recoil when I hear people say things like, 'That's an ideal, not real life.' Once we begin to accept the current standard as the only possible benchmark, we begin an inexorable slide to even lower standards.

Human beings are made to look upwards, to strive towards greater things. Social psychologist Jonathan Haidt writes, in *The Journal of Positive Psychology*, of a phenomenon which he calls elevation – an emotional response to witnessing acts of virtue or moral beauty. 'Witnessing and interacting with excellent individuals can create opportunities for enrichment of the self and society. Inspiring leaders, caring benefactors, and selfless saints do more than draw praise from emotionally-responsive witnesses; these exemplary others inspire people to improve themselves, their behaviour, and their relationships.'

There can be a great deal of ugliness in modern life, a tendency to tear people down rather than to nurture them, to ascribe the worst possible motives rather than giving the benefit of the doubt, to slam rather than support.

People fear the concept of service. They tend to associate service with its extreme and unhealthy caricature, being a tightly smiling but inwardly resentful doormat. Even the word service has been downgraded, to meaning primarily something that one does for pay, but freely chosen service is a vital part of a civilised society.

Service of others reminds us that we are not atomised individuals, but members of one body, who all depend on each other and on this fragile planet to survive.

For me, the concept of service is deeply intertwined with my religious faith, with my fumbling and unsuccessful attempts to live up to the ideals of Jesus. I see my life against a horizon of eternity. We are here to grow towards the light.

Breda O'Brien is a teacher at Muckross Park College, a secondary school in Dublin, and a weekly columnist with The Irish Times. *She is a frequent contributor to media debates on social, religious, ethical and education issues. She is married with four children and is also a patron of the Iona Institute, an organisation that promotes the place of marriage and religion in society and whose starting point about the family is that all children deserve the love of their mother and father whenever possible.*

She admits to reservations about writing about her opposition to gay marriage for fear of harming young gay or lesbian people, but believes that 'not to do so would be completely lacking in courage, and to bow to a consensus that is proud of lacking respect for the arguments of others'.

'And all shall be well, and all shall be well and all manner of things shall be well.'

JULIAN OF NORWICH (1342–1416)

PAT O'DONOGHUE

I BELIEVE THAT I was created with my own unique gifts and that life is about discovering and appreciating them. It is also about using them in the service of others, especially those whose need is greatest. The great Sufi poet Hafiz reminds us that we have 'so many unopened gifts' from our birthday. It would be a pity to leave this stage of life without even undoing the wrapping paper. Yet human nature and our particular experiences can influence that journey of discovery and appreciation, or inhibit the sharing of gifts.

I believe in the Christian value of delaying one's own needs so that those of others can be served. I struggle each day to put other people first and in the words of Francis de Sales 'to leave behind the familiarity and comfort of abounding self-love'. There are so many examples from the world of nature that show how death and new life are necessary companions on the Christian journey. 'Unless a grain of wheat falls on the ground and dies, it remains only a single grain; but if it dies, it yields a rich harvest' (John 12:24). This also underpins my belief that at death 'life is changed not ended'.

I believe in the grace of the present moment. The Buddhist monk Thích Nhất Hạnh describes this as 'an appointment with life, an appointment that is in the here and now'. Regrets and past mistakes that are not transformed often hold me in the past. Anxiety about the future fights with the reassuring words of Julian of Norwich 'All shall be well, all manner of things shall be well.' I believe that the greatest gift is presence – presence to God within, presence to self and presence to all created things.

Father Pat O'Donoghue is a priest of the Archdiocese of Dublin, Director of the Dublin Diocesan Liturgy Resource Centre and lecturer in Liturgy at Mater Dei Institute of Education. He is chaplain to the Redemptoristine Community in Drumcondra.

Colm O'Gorman

Life. Life gives meaning to life. A simple concept maybe, but one that for me embraces all of the joy and endless possibility of being alive in this moment, and the next, and all the ones that might follow.

I care little about the concept of an afterlife. I find it a terrible distraction. I grew up watching people apparently obsess about what might follow this life, and living in fear of damnation rather than in glory at the wonder of life as we know it. I always remember a few who, frankly, were not terribly nice, but who seemed to have bought into the idea that all they had to do to ensure their eternal reward was be faithful to the demands of dogma and authority, to please those who demanded their respect as a means of securing salvation, whilst at the same time they behaved dreadfully towards other, less powerful people.

At my core then, I think it is love, and being gifted the

capacity to both give and receive love that gives life its quality, its true meaning and purpose. There is nothing more tragic to me than witnessing someone who has had their capacity to love themselves and others brutalised out of existence or so suppressed that it dares not find true expression.

I am convinced that when my head rests on my pillow in my last moments of life my thoughts will not be of any particular accomplishment or professional achievement, or of the assets I might have accumulated. I am certain that my thoughts will be focused on a life hopefully well lived, as defined by the quality with which I have both loved and been loved. That, more than anything else, will define my experience of being alive, and give real meaning to my existence.

It is the seemingly small things we do that are perhaps the most significant. Whatever professional achievements I might accomplish, they, with time, will become irrelevant. Others will come along, and no matter how mighty my work, they will build upon it and my efforts will rightly become no more than a footnote.

But the seemingly small things will endure. The quality of my loving will be passed along across generations to come. My children will love their children, based in part upon how they have been loved by me. Their ability to love gloriously and freely, to hug, to cherish, to hold and nurture, will reflect the quality of how I held and nurtured them. And their children's children will do the same. And that will be my legacy, as it is the legacy of my own father and mother and of those who came before them.

That then, the seemingly small act of a hug, or a meal prepared with love and purpose, is in fact the really big thing. That is what gives life meaning. That is why I am here.

Colm O'Gorman is the Executive Director of Amnesty International Ireland. He is the founder and former Director of One in Four, the national NGO that supports women and men who have experienced sexual violence.

In 1998, Colm launched a case against the Roman Catholic Church as a result of his experience of sexual abuse by a priest when he was a teenager. He went on to sue the bishop of his diocese of Ferns and the Pope. In 2002, he took part in a documentary detailing the story of his battle with the Catholic Church. The film, Suing the Pope, *resulted in the resignation of the Bishop of Ferns, Dr Brendan Comiskey. Subsequently, in his role as Director of One in Four, Colm was instrumental in the establishment of the Ferns Enquiry, the first state investigation into clerical abuse in Ireland.*

BILL O'HERLIHY

I HAVE BEEN very lucky, blessed if you will, all my life. Blessed to have been born into a house full of love with a dad and mum who instilled in me and my three brothers and two sisters values and principles which have stood to me all my life.

These values, which included belief in God, the public worship of God through religious practice, a strict code of honour and integrity in my dealings with others, have informed my relationships with my own family and friends.

I have been blessed too with a marvellous wife, Hilary, and two terrific daughters, Jill and Sally. Ours has been a happy family that has strengthened through the years. I look now on my five grandchildren and I recognise how much my background has given meaning to our relationships and to my life. It has not *all* been roses but, overwhelmingly, it has been roses. I like to think the legacy bequeathed by me will be sustained by my daughters in their family life and that will make me both humble and immensely proud.

Ireland has changed enormously in my lifetime and very much for the better. Perhaps the biggest change has been the reduced role and power of the Church. With increased education and a growing sophistication among our citizens this has been inevitable and I have no problem with it. Clerical power has not always been positive and traditional blind faith is no substitute for firmly held belief. But what does worry me in 21st-century Ireland is what I term the aggressive secularism growing in the media and among some influential public representatives which, in my view, has damaged and is damaging the soul of Ireland.

What we have lost, in terms of the traditions built over many centuries largely on faith, has not been replaced. In some respects we are a moral desert reflected in a crime rate that is increasingly vicious to the extent that one newspaper complained recently that casual savagery was now commonplace in Ireland. Not to mention cavalier white-collar practice and negligent regulation that has brought the country to economic ruin. Yet five years down the line there is, to a major extent, little accountability; no one yet brought to justice for what are crimes, intentional or otherwise, against the people of Ireland.

So what gives me the right to the high moral ground? What have I contributed and, indeed, when I depart this life to the Eternal Life promised us, how will people assess my contribution? My business life through television and public relations has given me a certain reach but I very much doubt I've had any influence in moulding opinion on the great issues of the day. Indeed, if I am honest, I have favoured privacy over taking a stand; that may be understandable but perhaps it is nothing to be proud of either.

So how would I like to be remembered? Decent and honest, I hope. Someone who tried his best. Quietly.

Bill O'Herlihy's debut in television broadcasting was in 1965 with a programme commemorating the sinking of the Lusitania *off the Cork coast in 1915. He continued as a freelance reporter for RTÉ while also working as a journalist for the* Cork Examiner. *He subsequently joined the current affairs programme* 7 Days, *and was involved in controversy when hidden cameras were used in the reporting of a story on illegal money lending.*

O'Herlihy became a regular presenter with the RTÉ sports department. He is perhaps best known for his role as RTÉ soccer host alongside Eamon Dunphy, Johnny Giles and Liam Brady. He also covered major sports events such as the Olympic Games and International Athletics Championships up until his recent retirement.

MICHAEL O'SULLIVAN

WHEN MY BROTHER, sister and I were small children, my father would come and say goodnight to us when he came home in the evenings. One evening, aged five, I remember him asking had we said our night prayers, and I replied I had a toothache. Pausing ever so slightly, he responded I did not have to pray then as God would understand how I was feeling. Utterly unexpectedly, his words immediately impacted on me in a way that led to a deep, warm, peaceful experience. I experienced myself in my embodied consciousness being reassured, being cared for; I experienced that my pain mattered, that I mattered – to God. I experienced and understood that God was a kind God, and that this profound realisation was being gifted to me from beyond myself.

Reflecting on what happened that evening in later life has enabled me to identify this experience of spiritual consolation regarding the reality of God as a God of kindness being so powerfully transformative in my subjectivity that it became a foundational criterion for me in how to be an authentic human being. Whatever was in line with that experience could be trusted, and whatever contradicted that experience had to be rejected or opposed. For example, my decision to go to Chile in the early 1980s to tackle the brutal military dictatorship of General Pinochet, who claimed to be a loyal Catholic, was influenced by my desire to mediate the kind God of my childhood into the Chile situation for the sake of its transformation. Similarly, I have specialised in liberation and feminist theologies, and in the study of spirituality, because, for me, these seek to bring the transformative beauty, truth, goodness and love of God's kindness into situations of lived oppression. For example, when I read a story like that of Jesus and Mary of Magdala I do so drawing on the imagination as a principle of interpretation structured by my spiritual experience in childhood and the added input of my later studies. Re-reading the story in this way leads me to hold that, if we accept Mary of Magdala was endowed with a desire to live a life of authenticity, and was a sensitive and intelligent woman in a society and history that did not value her sufficiently as a woman because it was possessed by the demonic spirit of patriarchy and androcentrism, then we have grounds for holding she was suffering from socially induced depression when she met Jesus, a person of religious authority. His valuing of her as the woman she was led to a breakthrough experience at embodied depth where she met the same God that my father facilitated me to meet all those years ago when I was a child in pain needing to know God was kind, caring, gentle, and understanding, especially to those who were vulnerable. For me, being alive is about being with that kind God, and others, loving the world, and looking forward to being together eternally, eventually.

Michael O'Sullivan is a Jesuit priest. He is Director of the MA in Christian Spirituality programme at All Hallows College, Dublin City University and has campaigned on behalf of oppressed people in Ireland, Latin America, Africa and Asia.

He is the co-editor of Spiritual Capital: Spirituality in Practice in Christian Perspective *(2012, Ashgate). Spiritual Capital is a concept that is being embraced by a range of theorists in response to the great destruction being wrought by the global economic crises. It seeks to refocus discussion on core social values, on individuals' value systems and the internal dynamics that impel human beings to live by truth, goodness and love. While some scholars value spiritual capital from the perspective of the beneficial social influence of religious belief and practice, others value it more broadly as the value of activities which foster contemplative living, stimulate creativity, motivation and morality.*

GRAHAM PARKES

'WHY AM I HERE?' No particular reason, as far as I can tell. Biologically speaking, I suppose it's because my parents got together, then raised me, and I have managed to survive since then. It is amazing that all of us alive today have managed to make it this far, in the absence of any apparent grand plan. Indeed, it is amazing that anything exists at all, rather than nothing: definitely grounds for wonder – not to mention celebration.

This is certainly the strangest time I have lived in, for we seem to have succumbed, as a race, to collective insanity. It has been clear for some time now that our burning of fossil fuels is heating up the planet, and the change in the climate is already jeopardising the livelihood of millions – and will soon destroy many more, especially in the developing world. But the chaos resulting from sea-level rise, droughts and floods, disruption of food production and 'extreme weather events' will be global in scope – think of millions of climate refugees, and increasing numbers of angry eco-terrorists – and yet we blithely continue with fossil-fuel business as usual, to the detriment of future generations.

As far as meaning is concerned, I suppose there are three main sources: personal relations, enjoyment of the fruits of art and culture, and some kind of communion with the natural world. I have moved around a lot, and so regret that most friends live far away, since air travel is now such an unpleasant ordeal, and a devastating con-tributor to global warming. On the other hand, modern technology gives us access as never before, and at a modest environmental cost, to the riches of the world's great cultures. Yet at the same time we continue to destroy more and more of the natural world.

A life that benefits the world surely involves engaging in sane and creative intercourse with our fellow human beings, enhancing and propagating the fruits of culture, and trying to preserve the natural world for the sake of future generations. As for any legacy, I trust that my wife and daughter, and friends and former students, will survive me and continue to influence the world for the better. Having published a fair amount of philosophical writing, I would like to think that some of it will be read, and understood, at least for a while.

What life after death would consist in is problematic, since this life is so intimately tied to being embodied, and life as mere mind or pure spirit doesn't sound so lively. Of course, if you can persuade people that there is life after death, and that the good and the wicked will get their just desserts, it is an excellent way of getting them to shape up. But the idea of an afterlife, usually understood as better than or superior to this life, tends to denigrate the value of the existence we enjoy here and now. The apparent finitude of human life – the fact that we are mortal and so there is not much time left – for me makes those remaining few years, months, days, or hours all the more precious.

A native of Glasgow, Graham Parkes taught Asian and comparative philosophy at the University of Hawaii for thirty years before being appointed Professor of Philosophy at University College Cork in 2008.

Most of his research is in the areas of environmental philosophy, political philosophy, and philosophy of art, and mostly from a comparative perspective, between continental European and east Asian thought. He is currently working on a new book, The Politics of Global Warming: World-Philosophical Perspectives.

CONOR POPE

ANYONE WHO WRITES for a living is familiar with the tyranny of the blank page and I have been under its thumb for weeks now, thanks to four small words asking one big question: why am I here?

Honestly? I have absolutely no idea. This absence of an answer is kind of mortifying for me because I studied the meaning of life for years. Well, I say 'studied', but, truth be told, study was not a big part of my student days. I only chose Philosophy as my degree subject because someone told me it was a doddle to pass and I figured such a doddle would give me more time to smoke cigarettes and talk to girls wearing heavy wool jumpers smelling faintly of patchouli oil and rain in the basement of University College Galway. Which is what I did.

Turns out Philosophy *was* an easy course to pass but it was a much harder one in which to do well. I didn't.

Instead I graduated with a poor degree and was shocked to discover that pre-Celtic Tiger Ireland had little interest in indolent philosophers from the west. So I quickly shelved my handful of profound thoughts, figuring I would never need them again.

Now look at me, desperate for something wise to get me to the end of this page.

When I was a child I used to read a picture bible every night before bed – cover to cover – and I went to Mass religiously. In my head, the purpose of living was to die and get to heaven without sinning too much along the way. It was a simple – if kind of terrifying – philosophy. Then, in my mid-teens, I stopped going to Mass. God didn't strike me down as I feared he might that first day I chose the Salthill Prom over the Salthill priest, so I stopped believing – not in a zealous, Richard Dawkins kind of way, but in a more relaxed, agnostic fashion.

I have worn this lazy agnosticism ever since and I spent my twenties and thirties not caring about the answers to troubling philosophical questions, living instead for the moment. Money came and went and was spent on whatever ephemera I thought might make me happy. Sometimes it did – at least briefly – but more frequently it did not.

I fell into journalism, a job which, as English journalist Nicholas Tomalin put it, needs no more than 'ratlike cunning, a plausible manner and a little literary ability'. Then I got lucky. Journalists are not, typically, well liked by the public but I am spared much of the fear and loathing reserved for my fellow hacks because every week

I get to help people sort out their problems on the pages of *The Irish Times* and on the *Ray D'Arcy Show* on Today FM. They are nice platforms to have.

I mention this now because I recently got a very sad email. It came from a woman who spent last summer planning a once-in-a-lifetime holiday with her husband and two young children to Disneyland. Everything was in place by September and the deposit had been paid. Then her husband died in his sleep. He was just thirty-two. The tour operator will not give her the deposit back and that is why she contacted me. I hope to get it back for her, but her husband, the father of her two little children, is gone for good.

When my demons come in the dead of night tonight, as I know they will, I will think about this couple, and the fragility of life, and I will fret about my own mortality and what will become of me. Then, if I am lucky, my little girl will pad sleepily into my room just before dawn. As she lies on my pillow casually forcing my eyelids open with her small hands, loudly counting down the seconds until getting-up time and telling me how starving she is, I will know why I am here.

I am here for her. And for her slightly bigger sister who likes her own bed slightly more. And that will make me feel happy. And worthwhile. I hope I can make them feel that way too.

Conor Pope is a journalist, author and broadcaster. As The Irish Times *Consumer Affairs Correspondent he writes about everything from mortgage arrears to over-priced sausages and frequently comes to the aid of readers wronged by businesses. He is a regular contributor on RTÉ radio and television, Today FM and Newstalk and once appeared on* Celebrity Masterchef *but was sent home after inexplicably adding a field of lavender to an otherwise lovely dessert.*

Deirdre Purcell

Why am I here? At the risk of being facetious, I am here because my mother and father decided to have me! I think.

If I read it correctly, the subtext underlying this book is philosophical: will my sojourn on earth have been for good or evil? To answer that is not up to me although I can truthfully say that, like most people, I strive at least to do no harm. And to tread as lightly as I can on this fragile planet.

One of the questions under consideration here is what it means to lead a useful life.

I always have a problem with that concept. Is it misuse to live as a hermit in a cave? How do we rate the hundreds of thousands of writers and artists who never gain any kind of traction in the field of public acknowledgment? The life of a beggar holding out a paper cup under an ATM? The virtuoso violinist who, suffering from severe

stage fright, plays alone in his attic to no audience but the
crows on his roof?

And who decides? Who sets the criteria?

The music is the point. The living is the point. I am old
enough to remember when most families acknowledged
the existence of one or even more of their kin who were
classified as 'odd' or 'peculiar', who would never become
'useful members of society' never mind 'fulfil' his or her
'potential'. And yet they were well minded, their oddness
accepted by the people in their communities, their lives
deemed as valuable as the next person's.

Potential, happiness, fulfilment, usefulness, positivity,
all the buzzy, fuzzy states to which we are, in this age of
ours, meant to aspire, are absolutely transient and subject
to events and forces outside our control. I can be happy
watching two blackbirds scuttling across the grass in my
back garden, miserable thirty seconds later when I hear
an account of the tragic death of a young man, or of the
deliberate burning to death of a horse. I can usefully clean
my kitchen but know it will be messy again within an
hour. Equilibrium between joy and sorrow is what is
(mostly) on offer to those lucky enough to recognise and
accept this.

Unfortunately for me, I do not believe in an afterlife as
a sort of retirement glo-park, somewhere to which we are
magically transported along with our last earthly breath –
a place where all misdeeds will be overwritten by a
merciful deity. This unbelief means that I will try my
hardest to live to the fullest while I am here.

That being said, I deeply respect the beliefs of those,

I spent almost all my working academic life at University College Cork (UCC), retiring as a Professor of Biochemistry in 2011. I introduced electron microscopy to UCC in 1976 and worked as Director of the Central Electron Microscopy Unit for over thirty years. I have published about eighty scientific papers on the biochemistry of skeletal muscle and on applications of electron microscopy.

I have taken a keen interest in fostering public appreciation of science and pioneered the communication of science to the Irish public, mainly through my newspaper columns (*Cork Examiner* 1987–94, *The Irish Times* 1995 – present, *The Irish Catholic* 2010 – present) of which I have published over 1,000. I hope that my public efforts will be remembered as initiating a social change in Ireland towards a widespread interest in science.

William Reville writes a regular column in The Irish Times *about the interplay of science and religion. He retired in 2011 from UCC as Professor of Biochemistry and College Public Awareness of Science Officer. He has published widely in science and pioneered the public communication of science in Ireland, writing a national newspaper column since 1987. He published a collection of his articles as a book* Science Today: Understanding the Natural World *(1999, Irish Times Books).*

JOHN SCALLY

CHRISTMAS WAS ALWAYS the high point of the year for me – particularly 'Big Saturday' when we all went into town *to bring home the Christmas* and my sisters and I went to see Santa Claus. One year in particular stands out. Armed with a shining two-shilling piece, a gift from my grandfather, the requisite fee for the honour of receiving Santa, I took my place in the queue in a state of high excitement. I was very surprised to see a nun with three small children of the local travelling family who lived in a big tent by the side of the road. Every time I passed that excuse for a dwelling on my bike I was chilled by the constant chorus of children coughing.

A few months earlier a family of travellers had come to live a mile and a half away and been shunned by some of the local community. They were refused entry to some local pubs and shops. At Sunday Mass they sat together on the back seat of the church. None of the 'upright' pillars of the community would sit on the same seat as them. A few of the more superior parishioners decided to go to Mass in the neighbouring parish.

I was going to ask Santa for a pair of boots and a football. However, my plans were modified on hearing Santa's conversation with the youngest of the travelling children who was just ahead of me in the queue.

'Now, little boy, what will I bring you for Christmas?'

'Please sir, would ya bring me a nice dry blanket to keep me warm on the cauld nights?'

How could I possibly ask for two presents after that? I just asked for a football and did not complain when I discovered that I had got poor value for my two shillings when Santa handed me a cheap-looking colouring book.

It was my first lesson in social awareness. Years later I recalled that incident when I learned lines in school from a poem, 'The Stolen Child', by Yeats:

For the world's more full of weeping
than you can understand.

John Scally is Beresford Adjunct Assistant Professor in Ecclesiastical History, Trinity College Dublin. He is President of Trinity College's Theological Society which is one of the college's oldest societies, established in 1830,

hosting discussions on subjects such as human rights, current affairs, and social and environmental responsibility, focusing on the role religion has played in helping or hindering our development in today's society.

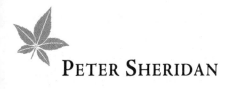

PETER SHERIDAN

'ALCOHOLIC DRINKING IS a low-level search for God.' I don't know when I first came across that phrase. It had to be post-1989 because that was the year I stopped. My drinking felt less like a search for God and more of a statement about self. I drank because I wanted to be free. I wanted to be wild. I wanted to be creative. I did not want anyone putting restrictions on who I was or what I did. My identity was bound up and defined by my drinking. I was wild and free and creative . . . and I was in terrible trouble. Deep, deep trouble. The kind of trouble that is impossible to admit.

So I did what many people do and I lived on in denial. The cost to me was substantial and, to those around me, profound. The only time that God entered the equation was when I was dying (hung-over) and in need of a cure.

God, get me through this and I will never drink again. Or when Sheila wanted to take the kids and leave me. *God, make her stay and I'll go back to Mass.*

I drank for twenty-three years, unsuccessfully. My father, on the other hand, drank all of his life, with no attendant problems that I know of. I wanted my drinking to be like his but it never was. He was my role model. I tried to step into his shoes but they didn't fit.

I remember feeling the power of whiskey when I was fifteen. My brother Frankie died of a brain tumour on 17 April 1967. He was ten years old. At his wake, a cousin gave me a whiskey and peppermint. I felt this incredible rush to my brain. The room started spinning and I held onto the table. Thereafter, I felt calm, content. A sort of nirvana where everything was OK. I forgot about Frankie and the pain and the awfulness. I was free again.

I don't know if my subsequent drinking was an attempt to get back to that place, but I have no doubt that the whiskey was my facilitator on that occasion. Frankie's death was the defining event of my childhood. It also represented the start of my drinking life. The two events are inextricably linked, but I do not think they are causal. I would have been a drinker had Frankie lived and I might well have run into exactly the same problems. But I do know that on a psychological level, my brother's early death gave me an excuse for alcoholic binges; and, in the aftermath of those binges, an excuse for my behaviour.

I would have drunk for many more years had I not started suffering from panic attacks. They finally brought me to my knees and to the door of recovery. I thought I was literally going mad. In my heart I knew that the panic attacks were linked to my alcohol abuse but I continued to live on in denial. I thought I could will them to go away, but they had taken up residence. I knew I had to take a risk. I could continue, as Dylan Thomas put it in his poem 'Fern Hill', to 'sing in my chains to the sea', or I could step out of the chains into the unknown world of sobriety. Oh, the fear of becoming a non-drinking bore. I took the risk and discovered that the world without alcohol was not at all what I had imagined it to be.

I started to attend Twelve Step meetings and these became my lifeline. I heard people talking about the 'gift of sobriety'. Not everybody gets it; some people get it and give it back; you can only keep the gift by passing it on; our fellowship depends on the spirit of giving, it is what defines us.

I met a man at a meeting one day. Known as Donegal Jim (not his real name or county), he used to drink meths from a brown paper bag in the lanes off the city centre in Dublin. It drove him mad and got him into fights. At night, he slept under a bridge on the Royal Canal, near where I lived in Ballybough. I often met him when I walked my dog along there.

Here he was now, sober. Doing a chair at a Twelve Step meeting. Talking about the higher power and how important it was to have a relationship with something bigger than ourselves. 'You know the difference between religion and spirituality,' he said. 'Religion is for people who are afraid of hell, and spirituality is for those who have already been there.' That observation has become something of a cliché now, but Donegal Jim is the first person I ever heard say it.

After the meeting, I approached him and introduced myself. He remembered me from the Canal walk.

'How's your dog, son?'

'He's good. Still alive.'

'That's good. He's off the drink, too, I take it.'

'You're a miracle, Jim,' I said, 'a living miracle.'

'No, we're all miracles. Everyone in this room is a miracle.'

He was right, of course. The compulsion to drink had been lifted from me and that was a miracle. The preconception I had entertained of the boring life of the non-drinker was being turned on its head on a daily basis. One small example: I had stopped kissing my father around the time I made my Confirmation. It was just something that had faded away. I often felt the urge as an adult to put my arms around his neck, but I resisted. Then I heard a man share about losing his father and the pain he felt kissing his cold corpse. I got into my car and drove to my parents' house. I went in. My father was sitting at the table, reading the paper. He said hello and went back to his paper. I called his name. 'Da.' He turned and looked at me.

'Thanks for all your help,' I said.

'With what?'

'Everything.'

I leaned in towards him. 'Give us a kiss.'

I knew he was embarrassed. I didn't care. In that moment, I had the courage. I kissed him. Every time I went into the house after that night, I kissed my father. It wasn't long before he started to stick out his cheek in anticipation. He lived for five years after that and I had five years of kisses – unembarrassed, beautiful kisses – with my father. And quite a few hugs, too. I had so much to thank him for and those kisses repaid the support and encouragement he had given me throughout my life.

I always thought that miracles began and ended with Jesus. It took my alcoholism and my journey through recovery to show me that miracles were part and parcel of everyday life. Donegal Jim was a down-and-out who had transformed his life to become my spiritual teacher. I learned more from listening to him than I ever gleaned from the men of the Church. He had been to hell and back and now he was bringing the message of redemption to others simply by telling his story.

For the first time in my life I experienced redemption, not as a distant thing or a religious thing, but as something present in the ordinary and the everyday. I was learning how to live from a group of ex-drunks. They were teaching me all of the important things, like having the courage to kiss my father and, in so doing, to show him that I loved him; and ultimately that I loved myself, too. All of this made me feel that the purpose of my journey here on earth was to become present to my own redemption.

Peter Sheridan is a writer, director and performer. His plays include Diary of a Hunger Strike, Mother of all the Behans *(from the book by Brian Behan) and* The Liberty Suit *(in collaboration with Gerard Mannix Flynn). His recent solo shows are* 47 Roses *and* Break a Leg.

MICHAEL SHORTALL

AMONG THE PROLIFIC output of the Kerry-born poet
Brendan Kennelly is 'Poem from a Three Year Old' (*A
Time for Voices: Selected Poems 1960–1990*, Bloodaxe,
1990). As a child is prone to do, it asks question after
question, finishing:

> will we have new people too to keep the
> flowers alive and give them water?
> And will the new young flowers die?
> And will the new young people die?
> And why?

Asking questions and seeking answers are fundamental to
us all. Therefore, the process of questioning and answering
will say something about what we are like as people. So let
us ask a straightforward question:

What are you doing right now?
You may answer: reading.
If you were to be asked why?
So that I may understand more ...
And, if like the child of the poem, I again
ask why?
So that I can get an insight into life . . .

Let us pause here and look at what we have done together. Firstly, I have to admit to a white lie, it wasn't any question. It was a type of question that asked about action, what you are doing, rather than asking a question about facts or taste. But let us look at what happens. Each question asks for a reason that makes sense. And in turn each reason is something you are trying to achieve, a goal. This is what you did spontaneously or naturally and you did so because that is how you are – a reasoning and purposeful person.

The questioning can go on and on. Some questions may be impossible to answer: did St Bridget have blonde hair? Some questions may just look like questions but are phoney: did St Bridget feel jealousy in her big toe? But the ultimate question about what it is all about, what the meaning of life is, may be described better as a cry from the heart. We ask the ultimate question because of the experience of tragedy, as the child of the poem gives witness.

So ask what is the final purpose or goal? The goals we are striving towards are the things or experiences we desire and so value. The ancient Greek philosophers and

Christian tradition answer that there is a final desire and so a goal that lies beneath all the things we desire and reach out towards. In other words, they say that, if I were to keep asking you why you picked up this book and are reading this page, you would finally answer: I want happiness. You do it spontaneously and naturally because that is what you are – a being that wants to be happy. Happiness in the Catholic tradition is called Beatitude. As *The Catechism of the Catholic Church* (1994, Veritas) reads:

> The Beatitudes respond to the natural desire for happiness. This desire is of divine origin: God has placed it in the human heart in order to draw man to the One who alone can fulfil it. The Beatitudes reveal the goal of human existence, the ultimate end of human acts: God calls us to his own beatitude.

Michael Shortall is a moral theologian in St Patrick's College, Maynooth. Moral theology is the reflection on behaviour and ethical standards in the light of the Catholic tradition and experience. His path has led him to work as a priest in Ballyfermot, Saggart, Rathcoole and Brittas, as well to study in Germany and Rome

He says that he learned as much from the people that surround him in his parish work as from the studies undertaken; learning to be work comfortably with people and to be comfortable with himself.

Through his work and study, Michael suggests he came to a deeper understanding of the movement of the Holy Spirit in responding to the gentle call of God. In time, he realised that it was not so much his commitment to God as how best to respond to God's commitment to him in Christ. In that light, each choice to respond to God would lead to another, ever deepening his journey to the point where a final choice was required – a final commitment to a way of service of God and his people.

PETER SIMONS

WHY AM I HERE? The literal and dull answer to this is that I am here because my parents met and had me, and I survived. We do not yet have a clear account of how life started, and I think there is no answer as to why it started.

We make meaning in our lives by what we value, positively and negatively. So I will concentrate on the things that matter to me, starting with the positive. My work as a philosopher, trying to work out the answers to difficult questions. The subtlety of the great philosophers, the brilliance of scientists and the creations of mathematicians. The wonder and beauty of the natural world, sky and sea, stars and galaxies, the variety of landscape and life, grand mountains, vast deserts and manicured lawns. The sweep of human history with its great and small actors. The miracle of great music, of those few who wrote it, Bach especially. The delight and privilege of singing in a good choir. The beauty of the human form. Unexpected facts. The majesty of medieval cathedrals. Imposing technology, particularly aircraft. The succulence of good food, the glory of good wine, and convivial company to share them. Family. Love and memories of love of other human beings. Pine trees above a lake. Italian hill towns. An English lane in summer. Hay and cattle on Alpine meadows. That rarity for me, a well-executed ski run. Cricket. A peal of bells. Shakespeare, and those who can act his works. Austen. Chandler. Churchill's rhetoric. The sound of the Merlin. Glühwein in the snow at Christmas. The Internet. Cats. Watercolour.

I know this resembles Julie Andrews' 'favourite things', without the rhyming, but that's just how it is. Like Bertrand Russell, I think we make meaning and find personal happiness in little things, private pleasures and small-scale sharing. Sadly, the things I most disvalue are not little. Not believing in personal survival after death, I hate life wasted, whether my own time trivially lost in watching and waiting, or others' lives. I hate cruelty to any being that can feel pain. I hate diseases, crimes and tragedies that cut off lives early and I hate the injunction to quietude in the face of these ills because all will be put right in the hereafter. I hate those who make others' lives miserable for their own personal gain. I hate all discrimination, because all people are entitled to equal respect and opportunity. Those are important hates. I am disappointed that the evils of the twentieth century have not cured humanity's aggression and violence, and that divisive religion appears as strong as ever. I want us to be more peaceful, less acquisitive, less corrupt, more rational, and more careful of our home. If we cannot, we deserve to be replaced. It would be good to think our successors could be less violent and wasteful than us. But I am not sanguine. They may just be differently awful.

Peter Simons studied mathematics in Manchester before being bitten by the philosophy bug. He taught in Bolton, Salzburg and Leeds before finally making it to Ireland in 2009, where he is Professor of Philosophy at Trinity College Dublin. Author or co-author of four books and some 250 papers, Peter is married with two independent children and one dependent cat. His hobbies when not philosophising include walking, skiing, singing with the RTÉ Philharmonic Choir and reading ridiculously thick and heavy history books.

PAT STOREY

'THE PURPOSE OF *life is not to be happy. It is to be useful, to be honorable, to be compassionate, to have it make some difference that you have lived and lived well.'* – *Ralph Waldo Emerson (from* The Essential Writings of Ralph Waldo Emerson, *2000, Modern Library Classics)*

Having a sense of purpose, to me, is one of the keys to unlocking happiness in life. When I first thought of going into Christian leadership in a church setting, it was to 'make a difference'. I still feel, seventeen years on, that this is my purpose. Whilst 'making a difference' is rather a blank canvas, in my own life it is demonstrated by what I have chosen to do as a profession – ordained first as a curate, then I became a rector of my own parish, and now I find myself a bishop! Yet if I were to lose this sense of purpose, I would find it hard to get up in the morning. I love the quotation above by Ralph Waldo Emerson, because it reminds us that life is not primarily about our own happiness, although I do think that God wants us to be happy in His wonderful world. It is about so much more – and perhaps happiness is a bi-product of these other things: to feel useful, honourable and compassionate, and to feel like you are living well. Do any of us want anything less at the end of our lives than to know that we have made a difference to those we love, and even to those whom we find it hard to love?

I was sitting around a table with two very good friends recently and one of them asked: 'if you were to choose one word to sum up your life, what would it be?' I found myself saying immediately: 'obedience'. They were some-what startled as I am a very independent and autonomous person. Yet my Christian faith, and the life I try to live, is framed around obedience to God. I follow His call – my life is no longer my own. This is not easy. Yet it certainly is purposeful.

When I think about the afterlife I don't see angels and harps and clouds. One of the worst things for me is to be bored – I fear that such a Heaven would bore me. Instead I see something purposeful opening up in the next life as I learn to surrender more and more to God. 'What do you want me to do?' will hopefully be a question for the next life as it is for this one.

How difficult it is to think about no longer being here, and thus the question – what have I left to the world? Is it a better place for my being here? Apart from the obvious impact I would wish to have on my husband, my children and my good friends, will there be a legacy that endures?

Whilst I do not dwell on this aspect of my life, it is significant to go down in history as the first female bishop in Western Europe. That was never my *purpose,* but it is fun to think that you have left something behind that people in the future will read about! On a more serious note, I am joyful that other women will follow in my footsteps and it will simply seem a natural progression without any fanfare. I suppose I cannot ignore that this is part of my legacy.

Of course my hope is that it will be so much more – I hope that as I learn to obey and to surrender to God's will, and live a life of purpose, that I will have lived usefully, honourably and compassionately. The fact that I am a very happy person in temperament is perhaps incidental. There is immense meaning in living a life of surrender to Someone vastly greater than you, who loves you and promises to care for you always.

Pat Storey is a Church of Ireland bishop and in 2013 became the first female bishop in Western Europe. She is also a wife, mother, sister, daughter and friend. She is married to Earl and has two grown-up children, Carolyn and Luke, and a son-in-law, Peter. Her hobbies include walking her golden retriever, swimming, reading fiction and creative writing. She loves to travel and considers herself incredibly fortunate and very grateful for the life she has.

'*There are only two ways to live your life. One is as though nothing is a miracle. The other as though everything is a miracle.*'

ALBERT EINSTEIN (1879–1955)

ALICE TAYLOR

The Journey

RECENTLY WHILE DISCUSSING the problems of life with a young friend she concluded, 'Isn't it surprising that there are so many sane people in the world considering how tough life can be?'

Her comment made me smile but also stayed in my mind and brought back the observation of an old friend when we were discussing somebody who was finding it difficult to deal with the result of their actions.

'We are not made of stone you know,' she observed quietly.

Maybe it is that part of us that is not made of stone that can help us understand why are we here and also help to keep us sane in this world. It is the inner being that lives within each one of us, call it soul or mind or inner being

240

that enables us to keep afloat. At times when we are in a good place it floods us with an appreciation of life and makes us glad to be live. That space need not necessarily have anything to do with beliefs but the real essence of belief can act as holy wells on the journey. It is the divine in us which expresses itself in creativity, goodness and delight.

'Vision or Imagination is a Representation of what Eternally exists' William Blake (1757–1827).

Our creativity is one of our streams of divinity and it enables us to dance with creation. There are also magic moments in life when all is well with our world. We see something that bring us to a breathless standstill – the first flush of snowdrops, baby birds fluttering from a nest, a glorious sunset, the return of a beloved friend. In these moments we are in a delightful world. It is good to be alive!

These are the stepping stones that get us through the rough patches and make our journey worthwhile. But we must look out for these stones and not be so absorbed in the mundane that we miss those uplifting moments that enable us to fly high with delight.

I will never forget my first sunrise. It was a beautiful summers morning and I was about ten years old. I had spent my first night up minding bonhams and at around 4am I went out into the yard which overlooked the Kerry mountains and the whole world was bathed in a golden glow and the dawn chorus was in full flow. I had stepped into heaven! The wonder of that morning never faded from my mind. My first sighting of Crater Lake in Oregon had a similar effect. Wonderful experiences open doors into the soul. As John O'Donoghue, the writer and philosopher, later made me aware beauty can wrap us in its invisible embrace.

Beauty in all forms lifts us into a zone that connects us to the realm from whence we came and to where we will ultimately return. And despite all the progress in the different fields of science, religion and technology we have come no nearer to penetrate that barrier between us and the world from which we came and to where we are going. We humans find that very difficult to accept! But in between those two unknown worlds we are on a journey.

Are we here to enjoy the journey? I think so and also to help other people to enjoy the journey as well. There is nothing more heart-warming in life than bringing happiness to another human being.

Most of us smile with delight when we see a baby or any new creation. It brings out the best in us. A baby is no challenge and no threat to anybody. It is complete in itself. All things beautiful are complete in themselves and lifts us into the realm of the divine. The wonders and beauty of life is part of the unanswerable mystery of why we are here.

Alice Taylor was born in north Cork and wrote To School through the Fields *(1988, Brandon Books) and other books about her childhood on the Cork/Kerry border. She now lives in the village of Innishannon in west Cork about which she has written* The Village *(1994, St Martin's Griffin) and* The Parish *(2009, Brandon Books). Her two most recent books are* And Time Stood Still *(2012, Brandon Books) and* The Gift of a Garden *(2014, The O'Brien Press). The countryside and the village are her inspiration.*

OLIVIA TRACEY

WHY AM I HERE? What a simple yet complex question! My instincts in answering are to focus on my professional self, yet life has gladly taught me that it's the little things that count even more.

As a child I was very much the Observer. I was fascinated by my stylish older sisters, Anne and Helen, and equally captivated by fashion, film, models, film stars and exotic foreign lands. I tucked away those observations very securely in my mind, dreaming that one day they would colour my world, and to this day my sister Anne is amazed by my myriad of memories and the details therein. Stories waiting to be told.

Though dreaming of a career in fashion and film, my rational side, along with the influence of family and friends, steered me towards a teaching career. But alas, teaching was not to be as I graduated from University College Dublin in the economically challenged 1980s, armed with a BA and H. Dip. in French and English, yet no hope of a teaching post. Though disillusioned, it is not necessarily the disillusion I recall, but more the weekly meetings in O'Dwyers Pub on Leeson Street with my equally qualified yet unemployed college friend, Mary O'Keeffe, and the hysterical humour we somehow found over a glass of Club Lemon as we bemoaned our professional fate in our new post-grad existence. Such comfort and richness we can glean from human contact with a good friend. It may not change things, but it certainly makes them feel better, and I believe that when we think more positively about our lives, our circumstances have a way of heeding that cue.

So by default my unemployed status prompted me to seek success and happiness in my dream job, modelling, which incidentally I began at the relatively old age of twenty-two, 'old' for a model, that is! I embraced every moment of it and to this day feel enormous gratitude for the people I worked with, the friends I made, the laughter we shared and the sheer confidence it instilled in me. It groomed me for Miss Ireland a year and a half later, followed by television presenting, theatre, film and television. It may seem like a superficial profession, but I believe that I both found and gave great joy as a result of it, not to mention the countless charities I got to support along the way. Still modelling thirty years later with Ford Models in LA, I believe that it is a path I was meant to take, giving me a career I relish to this day. I still get a rush when I hear the news 'You're booked' because in a profession where there is more talent than work available, I can't help but feel privileged with every gig I get.

I believe that life can be a tremendous adventure if we release our fears and follow our hearts. Susan Jeffers' book *Feel The Fear And Do It Anyway* is a marvellous mantra for living, and a book which instigated my long-desired move to the US. Looking back at all the places I have lived in and visited, the people I have met, friendships forged and the experiences therein, I feel enormous joy and gratitude for it all.

I also feel that it is no coincidence that the common denominator which enabled me to experience life as I have was that other string to my bow, writing. In 1994, it was a writer's visa through the *Sunday Independent* and its editor, my good friend Aengus Fanning, that enabled me to come to the US legally before winning my Green Card in the lottery. Along with my *Sunday Independent* work, I secured a column with *The Irish Echo* in New York and penned a few pieces for *The New York Times*. Most important of all, however, are the extraordinary people I got to interview along the way, such as Gregory Peck, our own Roma Downey, Gabriel Byrne and Peter Casey, who was an executive producer of the hit comedy *Frasier*. Likewise, with a passion for travel, I initiated travel articles and trips to exotic locations like Australia, Tahiti, Brazil, Argentina and beautiful Cape Town in South Africa. So writing gave me an opportunity to inhabit worlds I loved, whether fashion, film or travel. It also meant that my English degree didn't go to waste after all, like a piece of life's jigsaw that somehow found its niche. Today, I believe that I am still finding it, drawn now to explore the creative writer in me and recount my life's observations in novel form. I believe that I was born to be an observer and storyteller, and while I will continue to express that on screen or stage, I believe it is in the written form that I will express myself and inspire my readers most profoundly. I believe that writing is an avenue through which I will glean tremendous personal, creative and professional satisfaction.

Having said all that, I feel that I have learnt to dilute my definition of self in purely professional terms to find bliss and balance in the simple things. I have learned to make time to smell the roses, whether that be a picnic on a sunny California beach or an ice cream cone overlooking the glorious Ring of Kerry. It could also be an impromptu chat with a stranger, an exchange of joys and sorrows with good friends, a heart to heart with my favourite aunt, precious time with my ageing mother, or the urge to make up for lost time with a long-awaited love.

I have concluded that there is an inherent irony within myself in that I am a free spirit with a huge need for adventure, yet I am also a home body with an equally vast need to connect and create roots. The adventurous choices I have made led to many colourful moments, but at the expense of the traditional husband and children I'd always painted as part of the picture. As my father always said, 'Life/God works in mysterious ways' so I have no doubt that the future will bring more twists of fate and opportunities to grow and learn. If I could leave a legacy,

I hope it would read that I brought joy, light, love and laughter to those I came in contact with, and that I warmed and enriched their spirit as much as they enriched mine. At the end of the day, it is all about people, human connection and kindness.

Olivia Tracey (Miss Ireland 1984) was placed seventh in the Miss World and sixth in the Miss Universe contests (1984). She was a television presenter for RTÉ before shifting gears into acting. Some of her theatre credits include Cinderella *(Gaiety Theatre),* Lady Chatterley's Lover *(Olympia Theatre) and* The Donahue Sisters *(Irish Arts Center, New York), along with Hollywood film and TV credits such as* Gilmore Girls, Happily Divorced, Lucky You *opposite Robert Duvall and* Red Roses and Petrol *with Malcolm McDowell. She also models with the renowned Ford Model Agency in Los Angeles. As a writer, she was a columnist for* The Irish Echo *in New York, as well as being a regular contributor to the* Sunday Independent *and* The New York Times. *She is Ambassador to the LA Irish Film Festival and was honoured in 2009 as 'Irish Woman of the Year' by the City of Los Angeles and The Irish Fair Committee. She currently divides her time between Los Angeles and Dublin.*

Arminta Wallace

What it is to be alive

I'M BEGINNING TO wonder whether we human beings have been put on this earth to answer emails. Of course, I know we're all really here because of evolution. In fact, we are all here because, once upon a time, the dinosaurs were blasted to kingdom come by an asteroid, allowing small mammals to creep out of the forest and develop magnetic resonance imaging, car washes and Gore-Tex wellies. Evolution is a wonderful thing. But I bet that when he fine-tuned his work on natural selection and the transmutation of species, Charles Darwin wasn't thinking of mobile phones.

Yet it is undoubtedly the case that mobile phones are evolving faster than we are. Three years ago, my mobile was a useful, but not essential, tool. Now it has evolved into something more akin to a life-support system. It updates and upgrades itself without any help from me. It collects astoundingly accurate weather reports. It glides across time zones without a hint of jet lag.

Human beings, meanwhile, have evolved not a jot. We pretend to care about the planet while adding untold amounts of plastic to the Great Pacific Garbage Vortex on a daily basis. We slaughter ourselves and other animals with gay abandon. In just about every sphere of activity, from banking to biodiversity, we are way out of kilter. Aeons ago, when I was young, it used to be OK to stare out the window of the train or cradle a cup of coffee in both hands or, for heaven's sake, just walk around, hands free, in broad daylight. You daren't do that any more, for fear of missing the email which says: 'Did you not get my email?'

The most disturbing thing about this digital dictatorship is that it has happened to me. I'm old. Too old to be a digital native or a techno-whizz or to care about social media.

But not too old to rebel.

And so it is that on my mobile phone's camera roll, among the trees and sunsets, a swan on a nest (with eggs), whatever funny snaps of my grandchildren have been sent from Sydney in the past five minutes and a bit of video shot by accident in London when I was trying to take a picture of Westminster Bridge, there is a splendid image of an empty parking space. It always makes me smile – which is why it is there. It reminds me of my favourite joke, told to me by a real friend in real time. It's the one about a woman who is driving to a hospital appointment, and is late, and can't find a parking space. Distraught, driving in circles, she looks up to heaven and says: 'God. Listen. Please. If you help me find a space, I'll say my prayers and I'll be nice to people. I will. I promise.' Then she turns a corner and there, right in front of the hospital door, is a free parking space. She looks up again and says: 'It's OK, God. Don't worry – I found one by myself.'

I don't know whether there is a God or whether, if there is, s/he would enjoy this joke. But when things get out of kilter, it helps me to regroup. To juggle probability theory and spiritual ambiguity. To leaven the madness of daily life with the joy of sheer silliness. To give thanks for family and friends, poems and prayers, sisterhood and smiles – and empty parking spaces.

Four billion years of life on earth, just so we can answer emails? I hope not.

Arminta Wallace is a staff journalist with The Irish Times. *Her greatest achievement in life has been her beautiful daughter, Emma, and two gorgeous granddaughters, Ava and Abby.*

JOHN WATERS

WHAT DOES IT mean to be alive?

For me the astonishing thing is to exist. After many years of being fatigued by reality, I have reconnected with my innate capacity to be amazed by my own existence. I don't know exactly what it is I compare this existence with – some other, forgotten existence, some pre-programmed understanding of what is possible, even a sense of the nature of non-existence . . .? – but I have acquired the mysterious capacity to have this astonishment enter me at the most unexpected moments, sweeping me away with its power and intensity. In these moments, I am entered by the sudden implausibility, the ridiculous realness of reality, and somehow seem to know of another possibility which excludes it, an existence that has no beauty or colour or excitement – and this renders immanent 'what is' with an actuality that is all but explosive of my consciousness.

People sometimes tell me that it is strange to find that an apparently intelligent man continues to believe in the divinity of Jesus Christ, and to hold with the idea that the Son of God might have come among us to show us how to live, to die on the cross and be raised again from the dead.

I say that I agree with them that, from a certain perspective, this does seem implausible. But compared to the fact that I myself have come into existence, everything else is relatively credible. It is my own existence that I have difficulty believing. To be at all is the most incredible thing, compared to which nothing beyond me can be regarded as truly improbable.

The only legacy we can leave behind here is the witness of what it has been to live, and why this is precious and beautiful, and not to be feared in any way. This witness can take different forms. It doesn't have to be in books and articles. It can be in a way of smiling, a turn of phrase, a gaze fixed on the horizon. A useful life is one that inspires at least one other person to look beyond the constructs of humankind to the source of things. More than ever, we live in prefabricated edifices and landscaped spaces, where everything is arranged by architects and ideologues to steal from us our innate sense of transcendence. These constructs include the social, the political, the psychological, the medical and the economic.

I don't believe in life after death, I believe in life transcending death, a rather different thing. Eternity has already begun. Death, no more than birth, is not to be taken as a definitive moment of existence – merely another line on the cosmic, eternal path. (I almost wrote 'pavement' there, but that would be to place the path in the realm of man-made reality, and that is precisely where the danger lies.)

There are few things we can say with absolute certainty as unequivocal truths. But one thing I can say is this: I did not make myself. Another is: I do not make myself now, at this moment, writing these words. This understanding changes everything I have been led by the man-made world to believe about myself and my life. Something else defines me, and my life is a walking towards this Something Else, seeking all the while to put words on every step, so that others can see the path no matter how dark it becomes.

As a journalist, magazine editor and columnist, John Waters has specialised in raising unpopular issues of public importance, most recently the hidden mistreatment of men in Irish society, particularly in relation to legally protected relationships with their children. He has published a number of books and written several plays for television and radio. His most recent book, The Lapsed Agnostic, *is the story of his journey through faith, agnosticism and back (2007, Continuum).*

TOM WHELAN

FOR MOST PEOPLE, at some stage in their life, the question arises as to 'what is it all about?' Sometimes the issue emerges at a time of crisis or as the result of being through a life-changing event. In my case the question surfaced when I was living and working through a civil war that tore apart societies in two West African countries: Liberia and Sierra Leone. I was working there as a missionary, supporting a young Church and teaching theology. The sight of death, senseless brutalities, and people trying to survive after having had one or more limbs (or ears or fingers) hacked off by some rebel faction gave rise to fundamental questions. Querying the 'meaning of life' was no longer a theoretical exercise but had become an existential matter. If this question took on a new urgency for me through the war-experience, then an 'answer' came to be formulated through the very people who managed to re-form their lives in the midst of what seemed to be an utterly hopeless situation by reaching out to each other in extraordinary ways.

So, what does life mean to me? The God whom I am getting to know through the Gospels is, for me, a very un-god-like God – not a 'happy-clappy' one, nor a god whose favours can be purchased by prayer or a form of spiritual bribery. If we are made in the image and likeness of God – not necessarily as individuals but in our relating to others – then we can 'see' God in and though the lives of others. Not that any event or person captures God. Nor is it in the simplistic sense that God directs happenings. Rather I believe that God can be glimpsed wherever kindness, love and beauty are to be found. And, if something of God can be suggested by goodness, then it makes sense to think that God can also be touched in human pain and weakness. The Irish poet and playwright Aidan Mathews once suggested that at the moment when Jesus fell for the third time while carrying the cross, God 'consecrated' failure.

Our fragility and complexity as human beings can move us either to use others for our own ends or destroy them in some way if we perceive them to be a threat, or else to embrace them in solidarity, knowing the vulnerability and brokenness that is in *us*. We share a journey together.

Life assumes meaning and purpose when we accompany others in the ordinary events of life. Humanity is a gift and we need to embrace it. Relationships are complex, but are the very essence of what it is to be human. We cannot be properly human except through others. When we relate positively with somebody then it becomes a reflection, however impoverished and shadowy, of the capacity to love that is sourced in God. It is precisely here, in love, that we discover the place from where meaning is generated. And this love is expressed through care for each other, in the physical and emotional union of an intimate relationship, in the unassuming support offered to one who is feeling overwhelmed by darker moments, in solidarity and partnership rather than conflict and tension, and in the capacity to celebrate the thrill and delight that another person is experiencing. Basic to this is a profound respect for others that is not necessarily prefaced by or dependent upon agreed view-points. Meaning can be discovered, I think, in a realisation that our self-worth is to be partly found in our common humanity embraced generously.

The depths of the human person – each human person – reveal a mystery that is unique to each but also a sameness, because ultimately in our difference lies a familiarity and a shared humanity. Others know little of my life journey unless I choose to share. If I choose isolation, then my pain is not known, nor can it be easily alleviated. The flip side of this is that I can never fully know what is happening for another person unless they choose to reveal this – and even then I can never fully grasp the wonderful mystery that is to be discovered, through a misty epiphany that never fully reveals, in this person. In both instances the interpersonal process which helps generate meaning is stifled and can end up being negated. Society can create a culture that is dehumanising and which may promote excessive individualism rather than an environment that is respectful of a dignity and integrity to which we all aspire and which frames a sense of meaning for us.

A second-century writer said that the glory of God is a human person fully alive. We need to be liberated from everything that holds us back from becoming all that we have the potential to become. My belief in God often makes me look to those whom society chooses to marginalise, those whom it deems to be losers or misfits. In my movement towards the other I discover who I am and why I am. Ultimately, why I exist can only be explained by the existence of others and by my solidarity with them. It is enriched by their personalities and giftedness, just as I hope theirs is enhanced by mine. Those deemed to be misfits often have a lived life carved out in their faces in a way that others do not, and life's meaning, hard-won, inhabits their very being. My 'why' becomes clear in relationships, in mutual respect of another person's uniqueness as well as our commonality, and in our willingness to support and ameliorate human growth which ultimately finds its purpose in God.

Life is not a problem to be solved but an experience to be lived as fully as we can – and enjoyed.

Thomas R. Whelan is Associate Professor of Theology at the Milltown Institute, Dublin. He has edited a number of books and has published in both Irish and international theological journals.

'*The best portion of a good man's life:
his little nameless, unremembered
acts of kindness and love.*'

WILLIAM WORDSWORTH (1770–1850)

CATHERINE CONLON

I AM HERE to do the best I can with what I have.

As a child, I was blessed to be born into a large family with two sisters and four brothers in a wonderful home in Dublin. I was taught from an early age to do the best I could with what I had. To work hard in school. To believe in my own abilities.

My mother, in particular, never accepted shoddy standards and always expected the best. The best grades, the best in sports. I remember once, when I was in sixth year, she came home from a parent/teacher meeting. She had been talking to my science teacher about my entry in the Young Scientist Exhibition. This nun confided to my mother, with much mirth, that I expected to win it. My mother was surprised; of course I would expect to win. She loved to quote from Ralph Waldo Emerson; these are two that I particularly remember:

Without ambition one starts with nothing. Without hard work one finishes nothing. The prize will not be sent to you. You have to win it.

Dare to live the life you have dreamed for yourself. Go forward and make your dreams come true.

This last one has always stayed with me. Ralph Waldo Emerson was also known to say 'once you make a decision the universe conspires to make it happen'. The French philosopher Ricoeur similarly said, 'in imagining possibilities human beings act as prophets of their own existence'.

So if we believe in ourselves and follow the path of our dreams, anything can happen.

Winning the Young Scientist Competition in 1981 confirmed to me that if I wanted something badly enough, I could do it. All it took was hard work, discipline and patience.

Another part of living is being true to yourself. Robert Louis Stevenson, who spent much of his life in his sick bed, and so had the time to figure out who he was, said, 'To know what we prefer, instead of humbly saying amen to what the world tells you you ought to prefer, is to keep your soul alive.'

In recent years, as my children are growing into young adults, I am more aware of the person I am and the person I am meant to be. There is a freedom in entering middle age. No longer is it so important what other people think.

It is more important what I think of myself. Doris Lessing, in her discussion of middle age, says: 'And then not expecting it, you become middle aged and anonymous. No one notices you, you achieve a wonderful freedom. It is a positive thing – you can move around unnoticed, invisible.'

I know now that I love living in Ireland and being Irish in almost every sense. But there is one aspect of being Irish that I despise and that is our tolerance of alcohol and our ability to laugh at what internationally is seen as excessive and demeaning. Particularly in relation to our tolerance of excessive alcohol among young people. It happens because we allow ourselves to be blinkered about the damage we are causing: to ourselves, our families, our friendships, our economy. Socially, physically, psychologically, it is the single most damaging aspect of our culture. Unfortunately, successive governments have rolled over when it comes to taking responsibility for dealing in an effective manner with this massive over-consumption. And they roll over because they are coerced by the economic lobbying power of the agencies that are responsible for this culture.

I have a voice. I can speak and I can write. I have the ability to say 'No.' You may say that one voice is lost in a sea of noise. But that is not the case. Christine Noble, who grew up in desperate poverty, grew into a woman of vision, working unceasingly for the children of Vietnam and Mongolia, is aware of the ability of one person to make deep and lasting change; 'You are only one person, they said. But when I was a child, I needed only one person to love me. One is very important.'

SAOL

So part of why I am here is to be true to myself and to pass the best of me to the next generation.

I think I am here to love; to love life and the people in my life. In order to do that I must first love myself. Lorna Byrne in her book *Love from the Heaven* (2014, Coronet) speaks beautifully about self-love:

> No one is perfect – not me, not you, but if we loved ourselves we would focus on what we enjoy and what we are good at and we wouldn't worry about the things we weren't good at or feel inadequate about. We would be less critical of ourselves, less likely to run people down. There would be less jealousy, selfishness or greed. Our lives would be simpler and more joyful.

How do I love myself? By taking time to make little things beautiful. Christmas, birthdays, celebrations. My kitchen, my garden, family holidays. All those little moments in my life that are made special by taking time to appreciate, taking time to care. For me, that is a huge portion of my life and what gives me joy.

> *'Don't sit on the porch.*
> *Go out and walk in the rain'*
> KABIR (1440–1518)

ACKNOWLEDGEMENTS

WHILE I WAS compiling this book, one or two contributors wondered why I wasn't doing it for a charity. My answer to that was that there is more to charity than giving money. This book isn't about money.

This book is about finding something else – hope, understanding, clarity, purpose, meaning. About all of those things for the people who have helped to write this book, for the people who read it and, of course, for myself. And so, in this way, I hope to give something to somebody who is looking for some or all of these things.

To all of you who contributed so generously to this collection – I am deeply indebted.

To my parents, Delia and Peter, for always being there with a ready smile and the words 'so how did you get on?'

Everyone should have at least one sister and I am lucky enough to have two, Yvonne and Delia, who tolerate and love me in equal measure. To my brothers, Eamonn, Peter and Martin, who support me in all my ventures and Brendan who does so when he remembers.

To all my in-laws – Peter for being a bit of a madman, Patti and all the great ladies in the American Women's club, Noreen for being an angel, Kevin for coming to stay every Christmas (it wouldn't be the same without you), Geraldine for showing us all how to do glamour and Helena for keeping Martin in line.

To my school friends – Stephanie, Miriam, Fionnuala, Veronica and all the wonderful re-unions. My college friends are too numerous to mention. To all who made me at home when I came to Cork twenty-five years ago and accepted me as almost one of their own once I married a Cork man.

To all my friends and neighbours in Blackrock, especially my choir friends, particularly Jane who pulls us all into shape. Looking forward to Lisbon next year! A special note to Peig, much loved member of Blackrock choir who sadly passed away earlier this year.

To all my fellow runners along the edge of the Lee who smile and encourage and never make me feel the slowest of you all. Running is for everyone in every weather – for me it makes me feel calm, lighter and empowered.

To Ray, Abby, Luke, Conor and Charlie – read this carefully. You will need all of this advice and understanding in the years to come!

To all in The Collins Press for their advice and encouragement along the way.

Finally, to all those who have been a source of inspiration in my life: you are all here in some form or other.

PERMISSIONS

THE PUBLISHERS AND the author gratefully acknowledge permission to include the following:

Extract from *An Astronaut's Guide to Life on Earth* (2013, Macmillan) reprinted by permission of Chris Hadfield and Pan Macmillan; Extracts from *Lines I Love* by Mary Kennedy (2007, Merlin Publishing) reprinted by permission of Mary Kennedy; Extract from *Mama Tina* by Christina Noble (1998, Corgi) reprinted by permission of Christina Noble; 'A Vision of Social Justice for the Future' from *The Road Home* by Sr Stanislaus Kennedy (2011, Transworld), reprinted by permission of Sr Stanislaus Kennedy and the Random House Group Ltd; 'Think Carefully about What you Might Regret in Life' from *Flourishing* by Maureen Gaffney (2011, Penguin Books), how to achieve a deeper sense of well-being, meaning and purpose – even when facing adversity, courtesy of Penguin

Books; 'Where Are We Now' from *The Venice Suite: A Voyage through Loss* by Dermot Bolger (2014, New Island), by permission of Dermot Bolger; 'Patient' by Greg Delanty from *The Greek Anthology, book XVII* by Greg Delanty, (2013, Carcanet Press) reprinted by permission of Greg Delanty; 'Letter to Daniel' from *Letter to Daniel: Despatches from the Heart* by Fergal Keane, (1996, Penguin Books BBC Books) reprinted by permission of Fergal Keane; Extract from *TransAtlantic* by Colum McCann (2013, Random House) reprinted by permission of Bloomsbury.